Plain Anne Ellis

PLAIN ANNE ELLIS

*More About the Life of an
Ordinary Woman*

BY

ANNE ELLIS

UNIVERSITY OF NEBRASKA PRESS
Lincoln and London

⊔⋒

Copyright, 1931, by Anne Ellis
All rights reserved
Manufactured in the United States of America

First Bison Book printing: February 1984
Most recent printing indicated by the first digit below:
1   2   3   4   5   6   7   8   9   10

Library of Congress Cataloging in Publication Data
Ellis, Anne, 1875– 1938.
Plain Anne Ellis.

Reprint. Originally published:
Boston : Houghton Mifflin, 1931.
1. Ellis, Anne, 1875– 1938. 2. West (U.S.) —
Biography. I. Title.
CT275.E38515A32 1984   978'.02'0924 [B]   83-16835
ISBN 0-8032-1807-9
ISBN 0-8032-6708-8 (pbk.)

Published by arrangement with Houghton Mifflin Company

PREFACE

I WANT to assure readers of 'The Life of an Ordinary Woman,' who urged me to go on and tell 'what happened then' that I have written this book as soon as I could.

Especially have I hurried for those who could 'hardly wait,' or were waiting 'patiently,' 'impatiently,' 'anxiously,' or 'eagerly.'

And maybe you think I haven't rushed because of those who waited 'breathlessly'!

A. E.

'PLAIN ANNE ELLIS'

··

CHAPTER I

'The present is a distraction; the future a dream;
only memory can unlock the meaning of life.'
DESMOND MCCARTHY. (Rearranged by A. E.)

'O GOD — my God — God — God!' Hanging
head-first down a well, I was gasping this —
gasping and holding on by my toes and one
hand to the wet, slimy rocks and reaching
with the other arm, grasping at a baby hand
thrust up through the water. Twice it came
up, twice I grabbed, twice it sank from sight.
The next time — O God, thank God! — I
caught this hand, so small, wet, and slick.
And I held it; squeezed and held till this living
line — first, my fourteen-year-old daughter
Neita, who was holding and pulling on my sister Ruth, the mother of the child in the well;
Ruth, in turn, holding and pulling on my feet;
then I, my hair hanging and eyes popping,
holding and pulling on a four-year-old boy, till
somehow — we never knew how — we were
lined out in front of my sister Jose, heavy with

child, who, during this performance, knowing she couldn't help, had sat quietly, with no sound or move. She was on the job immediately; laughing, advising, heating blankets, and shaking and pumping water out of the wet William.

All my life I had wanted and planned to be a heroine. I had planned to do it by stopping a runaway team; this would have been really brave because I'm deathly afraid of horses. Now, when the time had come, I wasn't at all acting heroinish. Either I should have fainted or sweetly smiled as though this were all in the day's work, and walked nonchalantly back to the sewing-machine. Instead, I was trembling dreadfully. My knees had given way and I crouched on the floor, sobbing, and screamingly scolding Neita — my excuse the age-old one of nerves.

My husband had been dead but a few weeks and my sisters had come to be with me for a time. His death, like most deaths in my family, found us without money. Along with my loss of him was the resentful feeling that he had never had a chance. However, when there is a family to provide for, there is not much time for grief or resentment.

[2]

After his death the natural thing for me to have done would have been to return to the mining town of Bonanza where I knew the people and their ways. But Neita was in high school, and I was determined that she should go on. So, to support myself and children I was doing dressmaking, which was rather daring as I knew very little about sewing.

One day we were quietly working, I bending over the machine, Ruth pressing a finished garment, Jose doing lovely handwork on another. Neita was in the kitchen washing clothes. We were obliged to carry all the water we used from a neighbor's well, as we had none except an old one underneath the kitchen floor, used only for water for washing clothes. There was a trapdoor in the floor which we lifted and on washdays dropped down a bucket tied to a rope and pulled the water up hand over hand. Neita had been cautioned to close this door after each drawing, but this day had turned away for a moment. William, who was gluttonously cramming cookies in his mouth, strangled, ran for a drink, slipped on the freshly scrubbed floor and plunged feet foremost down the well.

When the scream came, I jumped and ran. (I take no credit for this because it was all done without thinking. I wonder if many so-called brave deeds are not done this way?) I went down head-first after him. Later, we tried this to see how I had done it, and with my utmost reaching I came only within three feet of the water.

Just after this episode, word came to us that our brother Ed, while in swimming, had been drowned. Ed, who had struggled and lived through untold and unbelievable dangers, dead? It seemed impossible. Why, just a few months before this, while attending a celebration in Salida, his horse had become frightened and had jumped over a near-by automobile and fallen on Ed, crushing and maiming him. He was taken, unconscious, to the hospital, undressed, his boots cut from his feet, and put to bed. In the absence of the nurse, he came to, and such was his strength and determination that he got up and dressed. Knowing that he would never be permitted to leave by the door, he crept out of a window, and went bravely — and barefooted — away from there, afterwards saying to me, 'There was no sense in staying in a hospital when I was only skinned up a considerable, and two broken ribs.'

Then we talked of the time when twelve or

fifteen of his cowboys, after the day's round-up, had gone into town, and in the middle of the night had returned well lit up and still going strong. Before turning in, they hilariously decided to 'chap' a certain cowboy. This chapping, as nearly as I can remember — if you think this twenty-five-year remembering is not a hard business, try it — is done by turning a cowboy over a log with his naked bottom up and spanking him with a pair of leather chaps. After the man had been well chapped, they grew warmer and bolder and concluded to give Ed a whirl. He, during all this uproar, had pretended to be asleep. They rushed him, dragged him from bed, but found they could never bend him over that log. Some one yelled, 'Put him in the spring.' This was the spring their drinking-water came from, but cowboys on the rampage care little about sanitation. Then Ed with them, they wrestled, rushed, pulled, pushed, tangled, and tore until they reached the spring; by now all were naked — and shreds of clothes were strewn along the way. Ed braced himself and went into action; he didn't swear, probably never spoke, but good-naturedly lit into that bunch of wild humanity, and one and all, singly, and in bunches, he rammed, slapped, soused, and threw them into that spring till they were subdued and sober.

Then we thought of a time when he was about fourteen. Some one in Bonanza sent him to Saguache after the doctor — there were no telephones then. It was a seventeen-mile trip over a high mountain pass. It was dark when he rode in. He summoned the doctor, then — of course he would have no money and would never ask any one for a favor — he tied his horse to a hitching-post in front of the Big Store and he and his dog went into the yard back of the store. In a hollow place there on the bare ground, they curled up and around each other and slept till daylight when the hungry boy, the horse, and the dog returned to Bonanza.

Our mother had died when he was fourteen and from that time on he never had a home. He was a child born without a chance in the world. As a boy, weak and timid, he was always 'picked on,' often hungry, associating only with miners and cowboys, and while he was with them, he was never of them. He never in his life drank or used tobacco. No woman, and certainly no song, had entered into his life. When he died he was a robust, handsome, self-educated man of affairs, having, unaided, pulled himself up, by the — no, not bootstraps, because often he had no boots — to a place where he was in charge of a large cattle company.

And now he was dead. His was one of those deaths that make you wonder why. We took him back to Bonanza and laid him beside Mamma on the mesa. There they both rested under the whispering aspens. This mesa is a spot beloved by our family from its shady kinnikinnick-covered places to the sunny openings where Indian tobacco and friendly daisies grow. As children we had all played there, each, with the material at hand, working out his own dreams. I, with small pebbles and twigs and flowers, built houses and gardens. To Ed every aspen there was a horse or a cow. He, as Mamma did, loved and understood animals. Each horse and cow had its name — each had different characteristics. One day, I remember, he called me from where I was reading — I always kept a book hid here in a hollow log, and many times when I was sent to hunt the cows I would come here and read. He was holding a bucking bronco by the ears. (To do this you had to climb an aspen, take firm hold of the top, then drop; your weight bent the tree over so the rider could climb on.)

This day I was no more than safely on, pulling leather, however, when Ed let go the ears. The bronco bucked, sprang straight into the air and threw me off, cracking my elbow.

Ed's was the first death in our family when there was sufficient money for funeral expenses. To poor people who are compelled to live from hand to mouth, sickness and death are, aside from the grief, a never-ending worry, which most people must go in debt for, a debt taking years to pay. Just a few months ago, I remarked to a relative, by way of a cheerful conversation, 'I'm broke. Flat broke except for five hundred dollars I'm saving against the time of my death.' He, a hopeful soul, said, 'Oh, go ahead and use it; I'll see you get buried; only I'm telling you right now, I won't use five hundred dollars to do it.'

Ed also left enough so that we, four sisters, two brothers, and Henry, each had several hundred dollars.

My dream was for a home, a stopping-place, a resting-place; so with every cent of my money I started one. I made my own plans for my house, starting first with a fireplace, then building around it. In the mountains near Saguache there are beautiful long octagon-shaped, lichen-covered rocks. One of these on each side and two arched above the opening formed my fireplace.

One day I heard that these stones, as well as those for the foundation, were on the lot, and I ran to see them. As I ran, I called to Granny Russell, 'Oh, the rock for my foundation has come!' She looked disgusted and said, 'Call that shirt-tailful a foundation?' It was a small pile, but a start, and I walked back on the lot to a place where the Sangre de Cristo showed rising above and between two houses, and there I told them to build. So from my kitchen window there was ever these mountains in sunshine and in storm, ever changing, always soothing, resting, and uplifting.

I had a large living-room. The ceiling and part of the sides were paneled in native lumber all stained a soft brown. Bookcase, window-seats, and china-closet were all built in. Between the two bedrooms there was a large closet with a window in it — I hate dark unventilated closets. The stairway leading to a large room upstairs was a feature of the living-room. Running full length of the front was a porch outlined with window-boxes. In the summer these were filled with nasturtiums which blended with the weather-stained shingles.

Some of my plans did not turn out as well as

[9]

they were expected to. No builder's plans ever do. Others were a huge success. My fireplace made the house cold, and, on occasions, smoked. To offset this, the cupboard was the best I've ever seen. It was a house full of happy memories. (I say was, because it is gone now, 'like a tale that is told.') Both children graduated while we lived there. Neita was courted and married in front of the fireplace — an enticing fire for the courting, banked with pine boughs and wild flowers for the wedding. Three babies have taken their first steps there; braced against the stairway as a start-off. All three, too, have fallen down this same stairway. And the happy, joyous family gatherings grouped around the old lady pioneer piano! — the first one to come to the valley, being freighted from Denver on wagons. People thought me crazy when I took her in and gave her houseroom. They never knew my pleasure in her low sweet tones, nor that to me she was a symbol. Oh, dear, no, I couldn't play; more than, when I was alone, to pick out what I thought sounded like,

> O, sweet and far from cliff and scar
> The horns of Elfland faintly blowing!
> Blow, let us hear the purple glens replying.
> Blow, bugle! answer, echoes, dying, dying, dying.

CHAPTER II

Sometimes I stop with half-drawn thread;
Not often, though — each moment's time means bread.
Old poem

WHEN I started my sewing work, I knew very
little about it; however, from the first I had
more than I could do, and during all the years
it never slackened — because of the fact, I
think, that I like my work, whatever it is —
sewing, cooking, politics, or — yes, writing.
And I tried in every garment made, every cake
baked, to give something of myself.

Sewing is like everything else — each day
brings its achievements, its disappointments,
its funny side, and its tragedy. I always felt
worried about my work until I saw it worn.
Many a time at a dance or a party, I have —
out of the corner of my eye — taken in all my
dresses to see if they 'hung' or 'set' properly.
If they did, I was happy; if not, there was no
enjoyment in that particular affair for me. I
would slip to the wearer's side and say, 'Your
dress is very becoming, only bring it back tomorrow; I did not get quite all the finishing
done.' I never made a dress to which I did not
give a personal touch, an embroidered button

[11]

here, a flower there, or bunch of French knots somewhere else.

I sewed good wishes and thoughts into my garments, especially so if they were wedding or graduation dresses.

I like hands — sewing hands, especially my own, willing and faithful. Many times I have been working on a garment — my ladylike, capable hands taking the smallest of stitches, my kind heart full of good wishes — while all the time my clever, unruly tongue, aided and abetted by my brain, which is no better than it should be, would be flippantly discussing the wearer.

These are just a few incidents brought from my garret of memory: A girl, whose fiancé had been absent for a year, fainting when I was fitting her wedding dress; and in a few days giving birth to a child. I felt guilty keeping her standing so long.

Another time I had sewed all day and was nervous and tired — this could be said of almost every day — and had decided to have a good steak for supper. So I stationed Earl, my son, just inside the kitchen door and said, 'Now, be ready; the minute Miss Doe pays me, you go get a good steak. No round or chuck this time. Get loin.' Finally Miss Doe came for the dress, tried it on and liked it, then gossiped awhile — all this time I was thinking of supper — then she got up to leave. She already knew the price, as she was one of those careful souls who must have all details in advance. 'Well, Mrs. Ellis,' she said, 'it was nice of you to rush on my dress so that I could have it for tonight, and you do look tired. Oh, yes, I can't pay you for a week or two, I spent all my money for new records.' It's to my credit I didn't scream; instead, I held onto the door-facing and laughed; told her I hoped she would enjoy her dress and that I knew she would look well in it. (It was red, and she had pimples.)

Another woman was one of those people whom clothes ride. And I heaved a sigh when I was pressing this particular dress with all its doodads and fancy touches — a yoke and half sleeves made of motifs cut from a heavy lace and appliquéd on a finer lace, everything outlined with two shades of piping held to place with French knots. Then there were three sizes of covered buttons, a design on each made of beads. These buttons were sewed in every place where there was excuse or room to sew them, till they looked as though they might have been shot from a gun. The crowning effect was a hand-made, two-toned, bunch of roses on one hip. When the woman came for it, I lifted it over her head, hooked it, and smoothed it to place. I could see she was disappointed. I said, 'That beautiful blue is just the color of your eyes.' She, looking in the mirror, cocked her head like a robin listening for a worm, and said, 'Yes, the shade suits me. I just like my clothes different, kinda swell. I only thought' — here she hesitated — 'you might have a few little surprises on it for me.' And I, knowing nothing could improve that dress except a good fire, said, 'Little rosettes up and down the front and upon each sleeve would be artistic. You have such marvelous taste — sort of Frenchy.'

There were several women whom I not only had to please, but their husbands as well. A certain woman had very large hips. On one of her dresses I tried to shade these hips a trifle, all the while she was 'juberous' (as my mother would have said); but the moment her husband saw it, he fired it back, instructing me to fix it; that he wanted his wife's hips to show. His wife said he thought other men envied him because of her hips. Another man who had to hook his wife into a complicated dress wished I'd 'sent a blue-print with it.'

It was a pleasure to sew for most of my

customers. One girl in particular was always very enthusiastic and got many favors from life. She gave much pleasure by exclaiming, 'Really?' 'Grand!' and 'Swell!'

Once a woman whose talk, as David Grayson says, 'was like a rabbit running in a furrow, no change except when it hopped into another furrow,' brought an expensive lace dress to be made. When I tried to cut it, I found there was not enough material; so for one morning I crept (I always cut on the floor) round and round that lace and pattern trying to get it out. This I did, finally, with only an inch or two left, and waited a week or more for the woman to come for a fit. One day she sent for the dress. No mention was made of payment for cutting or basting. Later, she did come and had a real fit. She said that I had cut it too small, and that I had stolen part of the goods; she knew because she had weighed the goods before and after bringing!

Sewing is like everything else, it has its good and its bad side — the good far exceeding the bad. I think one of the most trying things was, when women who were making over a garment would come for advice. As it's easier usually to do a thing than explain how to do it, it ordinarily ended in my doing it. There was one woman who would say, 'Now just drop your work. I want you to show me how to do this. It will only take you a minute. I've been a week trying to get it out. Besides, it makes me nervous; things annoy me, I'm so sensitive and high-strung.' I, trembling, weak with fatigue, would lay aside my work, which I would be paid for, spread her material on the floor and turn and twist a pattern that called for yards more goods than she had. She would then complacently roll it up, saying, 'Well, you did get it out. It's so easy for you; only it's not quite as I planned it.' To make up for this sort there were many who were especially kind, bringing cream, butter, and eggs. Two women were both considered, by their neighbors, to be 'near' and 'close,' but when I would tell them the price of a dress, they always added a dollar or more.

It is trying for every one, I think, to carry on a business in the house where you live. If you are tired, nervous, and worried, as the sewing woman usually is, you take it out on your family, or at least you haven't the patience with them you otherwise would have. If you have trouble in the home, you work heavy-hearted. Why, I have had to be pleasant, and, after having a round with one of the

children, smile when I could feel my face drawing and was full of tears inside.

The trouble with me, if it was a trouble —
and even now I won't say that it was the right
way — only it was my way, and of this I am
very sure, for me, the hardest way — the
trouble was that I had an ideal for my children
— that they should be worth while and somebody. And I never let them slip, so far as I
could help it by pushing, driving, encouraging,
coaxing — although they would say that I did
very little coaxing — and by example. I never
lied to them in my life; I never deceived them.
I never cheapened myself by having men
company (I like men, too). In sixteen years I
never had a man visit me nor went anywhere
with one. (Oh, yes, I could have! And, oh, the
dances I've missed!) I thought, 'Time enough
for my fling when they are grown up,' and my
fling has been — well, never mind. I never
went, and would not let them go, with any one
who was not their equal or more. Insisted always that it is better to be alone if you cannot
be with the right sort. (I have been alone most
of my life!) This is a hard thing to explain to
children. Once I said to Earl, 'No, you can't
go — they are too cheap.' Astonished, he
looked at me, 'But, Mamma, they aren't

cheap — they have money, and we are always broke.'

When I told them they had to do a thing, I never quit till it was done. Many times it would have been easier to do it myself. If I said they could not do a certain thing, I saw to it that they didn't do it.

For instance — in our town there was and is a custom called 'running' or 'initiating' a strange man. Now, what I don't know, and never could find out, is this — do men, the first thing when they go to a strange town, let it be known that they are Don Juans seeking a place of satisfaction, or do they ask where such a place is — as they do the barber shop — or does some one, giving them the key to the city, volunteer the information?

Anyway, this is as it happens. Nights, when we hear shots, screams, the wild running of many feet, men's voices and more shots, we know that some one is being 'run'; that some stranger has been directed to a house of ill or good repute — depending on how you look at it. Stationed in or near this house is the gang of wise-cracking 'runners.' Then — the entertainment of Don is broken into by a supposedly jealous lover or husband, who is on the rampage, talking in Mexican, and brandishing a knife and a gun, and — the chase is on. Never yet have I known it to be other than a chase with all these shooting, shouting men in pursuit. I have heard of one man getting on his knees asking for his mother's sake to be let live. Another ran so hard and fast, he had a heart attack.

I always hoped some grand night there might be a man who would stand his ground with a shotgun. I, of course, wouldn't want to see any one injured, but I should like to see them nicely peppered with salt.

I had threatened Earl's very existence if he ever joined these comedians. One evening he was out past his bedtime. I was so tired I just had to get to bed, so I braided my long braid, and twisted my front hair into curling knobs, undressed, and went to bed, worried, trying to rest. Never in my life could I close an eye till my children were in bed. Soon I was startled by shots and the stir of a run. I jumped from bed, grabbed an old coat, pulled it on over my night-dress, pulled on high shoes without lacing them, and sprang for the door, intending to rush this band of men and boys, walk up to Earl, hit him between the eyes — he was fourteen — and tell him, the men, also the running, frightened fool, what I thought of them, one and all. As I pulled at the door, it, from the other side, was pushed into my face by Earl. I didn't speak, but there in the dark, fairly jumped at and on him clawing, scratching, pulling hair, and kicking. He broke away and ran upstairs. I went trembling back to bed.

Next morning when we were eating breakfast, with no mention of the night's adventure, a neighbor came in and asked, 'Did you hear the running last night?' She went on, never giving me a chance to answer: 'Ain't it fierce? It's getting worse and worse. Last night the Kents went to a party, an' Grandmother Kent was stayin' with the kids an' this man run down their street an' was so scared that when he saw Kent's light, why, with a flyin' leap — never stoppin' for gates nor nuthin' — he cleared the fence an' ran in, almost scaring Grandmother stiff. He asked her to save him, an' she did walk part-way to the hotel with him.'

Earl and I looked at each other and grinned, then laughed, then fell on each other, fairly rocking in glee. The thought had come to us both at the same time, 'Suppose it had been the athletic stranger who had opened my door and whose eye I had blackened?'

In a way it was hard for a woman to rule a

man-child so completely, and stop short of having a sissy or apron-string hanger-on. I have heard parents say, 'He' (the son) 'must be in by nine o'clock.' Never could I see why a boy should be away from home in the evening later than a girl, and I acted accordingly. Men — good men, too — laughed at me. 'You're foolish — that's part of his training; he has to sow a few wild oats.'

'Piffle,' I say. No man or woman needs to, or is better for having sown wild oats.

CHAPTER III

Better to dream, awaken and forget, than never to have been a dreamer of dreams.

A. E.

If I succeed, I think it good management on my part — if I don't, that it is hard luck.

A. E.

I SCHEMED to have my children in every play and entertainment; then, after they were in, I saw to it that they were well dressed — not for show, but for morale, self-confidence and respect. Also, I saw to it that they had their parts; trained them till we were all worn out. No, I didn't know how it should be done, but I did know — instinctively — how it shouldn't be.

For instance: each spring our county high school held a contest. Neita had won first and second in the valley in declamatory contest, and was now competing in an essay contest. One day I was sitting by the fireplace finishing a dress. She came from school and handed me the manuscript of her finished essay, 'The San Luis Valley.' I read just the first two lines, then turned to the fireplace and dropped it on the live coals. I said, 'Now, Neita, you know as well as I do that that is no good and that you can do much better.' She cried a little, and said, 'I cannot. I can't even start it.' 'Oh, well,' I said, 'I'll start it for you.' Just say, 'In the beginning, when the world was young' — that was all she needed. While she washed the supper dishes she outlined an essay that won first place in Saguache County, first in the San Luis Valley, and would have won first in the State contest had it been sent in time.

If there was going to be a party and I feared the children might not be invited, I called the party-giver, offering to help, to bake a cake or make candy. I wasn't so much concerned over their enjoyment; it was the social training I wanted them to have. However, I believe in every one always having the best time possible, and getting all the enjoyment out of life one can without injury to one's self or to another.

In so far as I could, and with the help of magazines, I tried to teach them etiquette. Although magazines, I find, are more concerned with people who keep a maid than they are with the maid. When in doubt, I taught them always to do the simplest thing. Simplicity is or should be, the keynote of etiquette. Once Earl was going to a dinner party.

I Emily-Price posted him, telling him, among other things, 'Now if they have soup, dip it from you and take it from the side of the spoon.' (Right there my simplicity idea was knocked into a cocked hat.) When he returned, I asked, 'Did you have a good time — how did you get along?' He said, 'Wonderful! But say, instead of soup they had pieces of fruit served in glasses, and I had a heck of a time eating it from the side of the little spoon.' Once, when he was a very little boy, he ate lunch at a neighbor's, then went out to play, but soon came running back breathless. 'Say, I forgot, I liked that lunch. Mamma says you must always say something like that, whether you do or not.'

As I look back, I see I used a Spartan way, but I so wanted them to be worth while. At times when my way didn't seem to be working out, I have gone to bed praying for guidance. (This was before the war. I haven't prayed so easily since the war.) Most magazines had and have articles on the management of children, but evidently none of the writers had my children to deal with.

You will ask why, if I wanted to advance in order to help my children, I did not study and try to improve my own mind? This is why —

I was always too tired, so tired that I never read for instruction — only for amusement and to relax; so tired in body and brain I forgot things almost as soon as they were read. Many times I have read all of Mark Twain's books — he's a great relaxer. Today, as much as I should like to, I cannot recall a single passage. If, for any length of time, I had to go without reading, I was hungry for it. Many times when some one would be rushing me for a dress, I have stolen the time to read a chapter, returning to my work rested and refreshed. Once I was reading F. Hopkinson Smith's books — of course, always borrowed. I would read a while, then return to my sewing, my fingers fairly flying, my mind and thoughts in Italy. I stopped and started upstairs for something — still living in Italy — when a picture that had been cut from a magazine and tacked on the wall, because of its beautiful lines and lovely coloring, caught my eye, and — this I had never noticed before — in one corner was the name F. Hopkinson Smith. Why! right there on that narrow, dark, attic stairway, he and I almost touched hearts, hands, and minds.

Then, too, I was interested in and kept up with current events. There is no excuse for people, no matter where they are or how poor (because they can borrow, as I did), not knowing something about politics, art, music, books, and plays. I read all this because I enjoyed it — not as many do, just to get the patter; although I did patter, avoiding words I knew the meaning of, but dared not say. And oh, the burning hurt of having some one pronounce a word differently and, I presume, correctly, just after you have used it!

To see me, if only I were dumb — I mean speechless — one might consider me educated and well-bred. I wonder why it is that dumb animals show breeding in line and carriage while we human animals do — or don't — in speech. Just lately I met a woman pale of eye, buck toothed, scant as to chin, big of ankle and knobby at knuckle; but when she spoke, all this was forgotten in the music of her voice and the delight of her words — words showing generations of culture and breeding.

While we lived in what many would consider the most abject poverty, we never looked it. It is, I think, no disgrace to *be* poverty-stricken, but it is to *look* it. One Christmas I bought for some one a calendar; for each day there was a cheerful motto. After I saw it I thought, 'No one will enjoy that so much as

I'; so I kept it, hung it above the sewing machine, and on it marked every cent taken in. At the end of the year it totaled nearly five hundred dollars. So for one year, three of us — many times four — as my sister's two children were with me part of the time, lived on this amount. Yes, really lived — lived well, too. We never sat down to a meal in our lives that there was not a white cloth on the table, and always a bouquet of either wild flowers or geranium blossoms. Long before it became popular with decorators, I had trailing over my mantel, on stairway and walls, graceful baskets of wandering-jew. I am naturally artistic, knowing instinctively how to place a dish, flower, or picture to get the most good from it. Many times people who could have the things life had denied me thought my silence in the face of their possessions was envy, when inside of me I was shuddering at their poor taste. This was sometimes almost a torture.

When I am dreaming, I fancy this might have been the cause of this torture: I was cursed by some never-known ancestor. In my dream, he would be an overlord, intolerant, arrogant (often I feel his blood rising within me), knowing and loving all beauty and beau-

tiful things and sounds and tastes and smells.
Once a kitchen wench who also had fine feelings — they sometimes do, you know —
stopped her work, and leaned tiredly against
the door-facing with one hand on her hip,
the other shading her eyes the better to
watch the fading sunset. As she watched, she
dreamed her beautiful dreams of kindness,
warmth, and understanding — Here her up-
lifted hand was jerked down. It was the overlord, maddened by her slouchy clothes and
sweaty smell.

'Must I ever see you, find you fingering my
linens ——'

'Sire, they are so soft.'

'Looking at my pictures ——'

'Only the beautiful ones, Sire ——'

'Before this, I have even caught you among
my roses.' He almost shrieked and knocked
her down the marble steps.

She rolled over and crouched on her knees,
then, raising both hands toward the darken-
ing sunset, she cried, 'Sire, may you and generations after you be cursed! May you know,
long for, and love beauty — beauty in every
sense, and may you never be able to satisfy
that knowledge, longing, and love except by
the belongings of others. And may the un-

knowing taste of others, which you have to stand, torture and grind you into the dust!'

Then he, angry, impulsive, defiant, daring, turned toward her — 'So be it' — and went close up to her, 'But, woman, if I suffer through all eternity, it will be nothing to your suffering, because' — and he lifted her to her feet — 'because my children will also be your children. Follow me.' And she did.

Socially, I kept up, and each year gave one or two dinner parties and once in a while — a long while — an afternoon party. And I, in spite of being a poor card player, and never having had an operation, was invited to most of the parties. I suppose it was because I was a willing good cook and a sort of a town jester.

At many parties I would go and do the cooking, then go in and be a guest. This, though, was rather hard on every one concerned. I would sit trying to be entertaining while all the time my thoughts were in the kitchen, fearing the Mexican girl might not follow all of my instructions. If the food was praised, I was embarrassed — so was the hostess — if it wasn't, I was hurt. Then when I left, with the two dollars my employer had slipped into my hand, both of us knew I was lying when I said I'd 'had a lovely time.'

Once I was cooking for a hay crew. The cook house was quite near my employer's residence and it came about that she gave a large dinner party in honor of an out-of-town guest. This guest, in a long-ago time, had been my dead husband's sweetheart. I don't know how far this romance had gone — we wives never do — anyway, she had never married. But in her chosen work she had climbed steadily and had arrived. The day of the party, besides cooking for my fourteen men, I cooked most of the dinner served in the house. My employer, out of courtesy and kindness, invited me to the dinner. I, of course, could not be there, but I told her I would come in after dinner. And after my day's work was finished, dishes done, and next morning's breakfast started, I changed my clothes, and, with my back throbbing, my tired eyes drawing, I went to that party. I had to clench my hands and grit a few teeth to keep the tears back, but it was something I had to do. I just had to show them — especially this girl — that I wasn't the drab woman you'd expect. I just had to vindicate my husband's choice and judgment!

My children and I were always well dressed

— I'm not bragging — I'm only telling you. I made our coats, suits, and even hats, and how I hated them! Today I can spot a home-made hat or garment at half a glance, and it is never without a prayer and a heart pang for the wearer. Just lately I saw a small boy who belongs to one of those large families who only practice *at* birth control. He was strutting to Sunday School in home-made pants that were large at the knee and bulging at the pockets. I stepped behind a tree to hide my tears, knowing the love, labor, and misgivings that had gone into that small pair of trousers.

I wanted clothes. How I wanted clothes! I remember one sleepless night, tired from sewing on other people's clothes, I planned what I should buy, if, by some stroke of fortune, I became possessed of sixty dollars. With this I outfitted myself from head to heel... then slept.

People gave me their old clothes. These I would turn and dye till often they looked better than when new.

Here I will tell of an incident in my sewing days.

Over half of our population is Mexican — a kindly, patient, much-put-upon people holding onto many of their old customs and traditions.

They have a secret lodge or association called the Penitentes. No white man (we use this word 'white' to designate ourselves — we shouldn't, but we can't say 'American' because the Mexicans were really the first Americans) — although many say they do — and no Mexican, unless he belongs to the order, knows what they do at their meetings.

This is all I know. Each year, a week before Easter, they whip themselves. (Not a bad idea at all; I know lots of people who, oftener than once a year, need a good whipping.) Once when I was sewing at a rancher's near a small Mexican settlement, we decided to watch the Penitentes. At daylight the morning before Easter some one climbed on the roof and saw the Mexicans marching. We got into a car and went as close as we dared — I felt as guilty as though I had slipped in to watch some one secretly praying. They were led by a huge figure dressed in black robes. He had a wonderful voice and was chanting or singing the most impressive and soul-lifting thing I've ever heard. Following him were several men dressed only in light underwear. All were masked — they were bending beneath the weight of a huge cross. These were followed by others barefoot marching over the stones and cactus. Each one carried a whip of yucca. And as they marched behind this noble front figure, at each step and rhythm they lashed themselves, first over one shoulder, then over the other, and at each whip crack the blood showed through their underwear, in some cases ran down. And as the sun was coming up over the Sangre de Cristo range, we turned homeward, the silence broken only by a brave and hopeful first robin.

And did I have no thoughts beyond my children and work? Of course I did. I thought and dreamed of men. In the beginning I thought — and this thought kept me going through a good many lean years — that sometime I should marry, but as the years passed, no one asked me that I cared enough about to make the struggle against poverty with. And in our town there was no rich man who wanted me. One time a woman who let no matrimonial grass grow under her feet said to me, 'Here you sit on your behind growing old; why don't you get out and catch some cattle king?' And I did consider advertising, but could not afford enough space to tell of all my good qualities nor what I expected in a man; besides, no man that would have suited me would have been reading matrimonial ads. Christopher Morley wonders why in all Orange Blossom Band advertisements the writers say they are lonely and never tell whether they enjoy reading. The question seems to me to answer itself: if they enjoyed reading they would not be lonely.

I was often lonely and many times longed for the society of men. (Just the other day I was talking to a man who has known — I mean been acquainted with — me for over twenty years. He said, rather resentfully, 'Why were you all those years so secretive? We never knew you.') And how I did want to write to, and get letters from, a man! I often thought how I'd write him in my letters, telling him far more than if I'd been with him: tell him of my ambitions, my hopes, my aspirations, of my likes and dislikes. You see, I could tell with my pen things I would never give voice to.

But in spite of all my dreams, this was the real reason that no man interested me: I always expected Jim, my childhood lover, to return. Some days this thought and wish used to come so strongly that I felt sure the day had come and I dressed for him. Then I would picture the scene: I would open the door when he knocked. He would be surprised to see what a clever home I have and how young I look after all this time. I would say, 'Is it you?' and would glance at his hands to make sure. We would be married at once, he would be so impatient — so many wasted years. Then I would bundle up every stitch of sewing in the house and send it home to the owners. Then we would go to Denver and into the stores, and oh! the clothes I would buy and the presents I would get for all my friends! As I sat there sewing, I would see my children put through the best schools; I would have a lovely home with a big warm dining-room in which every hour of the day the sun was shining through windows filled with flowers, and there was a table set three times a day with fine linen, silver, and china, and every good thing to eat ——

But then it would grow dark and I would get up and have my tea and toast, which I enjoyed and was no worse off for all my dreaming. I think all women if unmarried — no matter how old — dream of the man coming and the comforts of a home, never losing hope; at least I do — and I don't.

And so the days and years passed. Neita finished the four-year high-school course in three years, and the summer she was sixteen she taught a summer school. The following summer she taught in the mountains, living by herself two miles from any other person. One day and night she was kept in her cabin by a drunken man lying up against the outside of her door — but that's *her* story. We planned and saved and were making the utmost effort for her to go to college. She had won a scholarship at the Agricultural College, and we thought with that, her clothes, all of which I made, and by working her way — it all sounded easy — she could pull through. I should have planned to go with her, but I was afraid. One day she said to me, 'Mamma, why don't you leave this place? You are too big for it.' I laughed — not, however, as much as the neighbors would had they overheard her — and answered, 'No, I'm not; if I were I shouldn't be here. And, besides, I can't let loose long enough to take hold.'

I speak of my children only where necessary — not because they weren't the biggest thing in my life — always my first and last thought; the directing motive of my every action, as they always will be; ruling my life completely, but never me. I think only an individual has the right to turn himself inside out.

So with her scholarship and some good clothes, all made by me, and a lot of courage, Neita started to college, intending to work for her board and room. I felt we were coming on, and when she made the Dramatic Club, I bragged a good deal; but she did not make a sorority, which meant nothing to me, but seemed to worry her. Then I began to notice, even at home, that it did make a difference. Now, when other women would monopolize the conversation, telling what their children were doing in school, I, too, could take a hand because no one did better in school than Neita. Then they would take the wind out of my sails by asking, 'Has she had a bid from a sorority?'

At Christmas-time I made big preparations for home-coming. Of course we couldn't afford this, but for one time in my life I wanted to be like other people — I wanted to hear, 'How well Neita looks!' and, 'I like the new way she does her hair!' and, 'Somehow she is different — college certainly does make a difference.' I planned new clothes for her and decided to give a party during the holidays and was making my preparations. I had my white and dark fruit cake made, also my candy and salted nuts. Then on the day she was to be at home, a telegram came; instead, she was in the hospital, very sick. I was crushed; I went into the back yard underneath the sky and fought it out with myself. Somehow air and sky help me to control myself; I guess they bring to me the fact that after all in the big scheme I don't count much. Anyway, Nature comforts me and helps me to say, like Lincoln, 'This, too, shall pass away.'

I went into the house and packed up part of the good things — cakes, date bread, mint jelly, orange marmalade, candy and nuts; also her new clothes, and sent them to her. I wrote her this letter (I found it only lately when I was going through some old letters):

MY DEAR NEITA,

I know I haven't written you often, but I have been so sad and bitter against fate that I knew it would do me no good to write letters and you less to get them. Am better now and am going on at the same old gait and hoping and wishing as usual, and of course dreaming a little as usual. Am going on with the dinner, but it's just to put up a bold front to the others, as I will have no heart in it.

Now, Neita, I have asked you several times of your plans and you must make some. It is all right to say, 'Take no thought of the morrow,' but it doesn't pan out. As far as I can see, you must be broke, and may have to come home. I can give you enough for two months, one now and one after I save it, and, believe me, it will hurt me as much for you to come as it will you. Next winter I will go with you. I had to fight myself again yesterday when all the girls came home for the holidays. I think of you every minute I am awake and try to plan or see a way for us.

And, Neita, I want to tell you again — don't dare pretend we are something we are not. I am afraid you might lead people to think we are something which we're not — and never will be, only through you or me. It has always been a wish and a dream of mine to found a cultured family, a family that does things; but it must be on a solid foundation and not one of make-believe. I know you will have no idea of what I am driving at — I do wish I could express myself.

Be very thankful to all those people who are kind to you, but don't take favors any longer than you can help.

With love

MAMA

We managed so that she stayed at college

until March, doing very well in school, also helping with that year's 'Silver Spruce.' Then we decided that she must come home. I had managed things so that she was to teach a summer country school. She had scarcely money enough to get home on — but this is the way we are: before coming home she wanted to go to the Junior Prom, so she went to a bank and borrowed twenty-five dollars to buy an evening dress. I don't know what she told the banker, probably that she wished to go to her grandmother's funeral. We fully expected that the following fall she would return to Fort Collins, but she didn't.

CHAPTER IV

Courage is fear anæsthetized.
A. E.

At this time my brother-in-law was the fore-man of a Government telephone construction gang. I persuaded him to take me along as cook. I wanted and needed a vacation. Then, too, by doing this work I could save more than I could by many months of sewing; moreover, the line was to be all over the high country. I have a passionate love for nature — the wilder the better. I can think of nothing that makes me so happy as to climb a mountain or a cliff of rocks. I am always tempted to see what is just around the turn in the road. And I love to cook. Why will people call cooking a menial task? — when it is the art of arts, and a good cook is a genius whose price is above rubies; who handles, daily, expensive materials, which, properly prepared, are the foundation of life and of all achievement. Of course I think to waste good food by poor cooking is a crime and should be punished as such. I am writing this just before dinner and, according to my system, the cook should be shot at sunrise. To cook, and to do it well, every talent must be used; the strength of a prize-fighter, the imagination of a poet, the brain of an empire builder, the patience of Job, the eye and the touch of an artist, and, to turn your mistakes into edible assets, the cleverness of a politician. Every day I hear women ranting about prohibition, who have, with their poor cooking, set up stills in their husbands' stomachs.

The Government is a good provider. It never refused to get any groceries which I ordered excepting dates and nuts. These I got anyway, by putting them on the bill as bacon. Our grocery list, enough to do for the job, was submitted to different grocers, naturally going to the lowest bidder. On this job there were ten to twelve men, myself, and Earl. To haul us and our equipment, there were four teams and wagons including the Government mules and truck. Jumbo, one of these mules, was the best-looking and the most dignified individual in the outfit.

There was the foreman, strong, kindly, efficient, doing three men's work; never saying, 'Go on'; always, 'Come on.' He was slightly deaf — unless you happened to be saying something you didn't want him to hear.

There were two old men, Dad and Bill; Dad a better talker than worker; Bill quieter, a dogged worker, and utterly dependable. They jawed each other and got along in a cat-and-dog manner. There were several young men. I remember only that they were good-natured and good eaters. There was Slim, a teamster, a hard worker with a sweet disposition; a Mexican we called Primo (cousin), quiet, clean, lovable. Another Mexican was Juan, of the melting voice. They said that in the early days a handsome, white, very intellectual lawyer from New York had passed our way. In transit he visited a Mexican girl and that day's good deed has given us, up to date, three generations of unusual Mexicans — better-looking, better-bred, more intelligent, and, I believe, unhappier, because mixed blood wars under the skin. All these men were kind and thoughtful of me, many times helping me with the dishes after doing their own day's work. They all brought, in their cracked, work-calloused hands, flowers they knew I would like. I have known them to leave whatever they happened to be doing and call me to look at a sunset. They all brought offerings of pitch gum, taken from their pockets with bits of string and tobacco clinging to it.

Our equipment was loaded the day before we started — tents, tools, rolls of wire, provisions, grain, hay, stoves, bedding, blacksmith outfit, big tanks, and so on, and next morning we were off. I think the men weren't any too keen over having a woman as cook. They probably thought Mrs. Ellis was all right to do fancy things for parties, but a camp cook was something different. This first day we left town in a rain, making only seven miles before noon. We stopped for dinner at a ranch and drove in under the cattle sheds which were leaking rain and dirt at every crack. The men cleared away the cow-piles to make a place for the fire, and then looked at me. I knew I was on trial and laughed and joked while getting the two huge coffee-pots on the fire. This did not impress them very much, but when I poured into a large kettle the chile-con-carne that I had made the day before, they began to take notice. When it was piping hot, I opened a box of crackers and we dined. For dessert, I gave them fresh doughnuts fried the evening before. Hot chile, coffee, and doughnuts made a lunch that on a cold, rainy day hit the spot. I had won my spurs — and spoons.

And did I fear being out with these men? Heavens, no! I did not dare, accept, challenge, or invite attention, so I did not get it. And did I have a gun to protect myself with? I should say not. I am afraid of guns and am not afraid of men. Besides, a woman who cannot protect herself without a gun cannot protect herself with one. Then, too, I find that in men stomach hunger is much stronger than sex hunger, and when it comes to ruining a good cook or a good meal, in most cases the cook will have to wait.

It took us two days' travel to make Los Pinos, where we established camp. Our cavalcade was always led by the Government mules. Jumbo was temperamental and refused to work if there was a team in front. So in the lead he and his mate went, the sun flashing from the brass-studded 'U. S.' on their harness and from the big brass knobs on the hames. All the way we had talked of Jumbo's tantrums, and when we were within a mile of camp, the teamster began to brag that at last Jumbo knew his master. But going up a little rise, Jumbo went into action or, rather, didn't. He stopped dead; the heavily loaded wagon started to back down and into the closely following teams. There was no room to turn out. It was a jam of plunging horses and swearing men. We all jumped — none quicker than I. And the fight was on. Every man there tried his hand at getting Jumbo to move, each — except Primo offered suggestions, such as building a fire under him, pouring water into his ears, and so on. All this time he was being urged, sworn at, and beaten unmercifully, but he refused to budge. It looked as though we were there for the night.

Then the forest supervisor, another brother-in-law, handsome, good-natured, masterful with horses, rode up. He took in everything at a glance, then dismounted from his horse, climbed on the heavily loaded wagon, took the lines in one hand and the long blacksnake whip in the other. He seemed to give strength to the whole outfit, as he stood, legs apart, his hat off, cutting and cracking that whip through the air, around, over, and into Jumbo, who seemed to realize that this was something different. He lunged, snorted, kicked, screamed, and jumped over on the other mule; with the knobs of the hames snapping and the harness ripping. Then, with one long, swooping movement, the supervisor, whip in hand, was over on Jumbo's back, swearing, whipping, lashing, and spurring that mule from ear to tail. Jumbo was surprised and came to earth, then, with the supervisor still riding, he lunged forward into the collar, dragging, with the help of the sweating men pushing on each wheel, the heavy wagon to the hilltop. All were relieved, I think none so much as Jumbo and the cook.

Our first camp, Los Pinos, was a few miles above the old Ute Indian Agency, and often, as I looked from my tent door, in fancy I could see the Indians, much the same as R. B. Townshend writes of seeing them in 'A Tenderfoot in Colorado.' Mr. Townshend, General McCook — the Governor of Colorado Territory — some soldiers, and a writer for 'Harper's Magazine' had gone to the agency. They had stopped in Saguache and taken Godfrey's wife, who was part Indian, with them. Her baby had died the night before. This is Townshend's description of their visit:

'The new agency, where our cook tent stood, was in a natural park on the Gunnison. The first frosts had painted yellow and scarlet the quaking asp and dwarf oak that grew along the gulches. Every hilltop was crowned with the tall red-stemmed columns of the pines, while the rich bunch grass clothed all the slopes. The cone-shaped tepees of the Utes stood in clusters, each band grouped, as its sub-chief chose, near wood and water. Naked

Indian boys were driving wiry ponies back and forth through the grass, while other boys were coming up from the stream with strings of splendid trout, and the gayly dressed bucks rode in from the hills with dripping red lumps of fresh-killed venison and elk meat hanging from their saddles.

'There were enough of them. The sawmill men swore they had counted five hundred tepees, and every frontiersman knows each tepee counts for at least two warriors. The new agency was being built in the very middle of the park, and here the sawmill had been started, and the wagons set to hauling logs to be sawn into timber to build with. This was a true sign of the white man's foot. Already, mutilated tree-stumps stood where noble pines had been, yellow sawdust floated down the clear stream — the sawdust that kills the trout — and raw yellow skeleton buildings of unseasoned boards were being hammered together by clattering carpenters. No wonder the wild Uncompagres felt the desecration and shouted for war. Yet over the wild Indians who had never seen a white man the General's word had power. He summoned the reluctant chiefs to council, and they came. The debate was long and fierce, for the mountain warriors were stubborn. I looked at the ring of savage faces, and it seemed certain they would never yield.

'What were the feelings of the woman who sat there interpreting their threats to the General and giving back his diplomatic answers to the savages in their own tongue? To have a woman so much as come into council with warriors was gall to the proud Utes. Did her heart quake? Well she knew how the Utes held us all in the hollow of their hand; and she knew, too, what her fate would be if they captured her. The Utes spare no horror to their captives. Her husband might keep his last bullet for himself. Would he keep the last but one for her? Perhaps it was well that her baby was safe in its little grave!

'But if these were her thoughts, the Indian blood in her enabled her to keep them well concealed. To and fro the tide of argument flowed. When the Uncompagres grew too insolent, and threatened us openly, the General answered: "You may kill me and my ten men, but there are ten thousand more behind us, and ten times ten thousand behind them. Ouray has seen them. Ask him."

'The General's confidence in Ouray, publicly testified, carried weight; the Uncompagres listened, and at last they gave way. They would accept the treaty; the pipe of peace was passed around, and we all breathed freely again. But the sawmill men, with the Western man's curious way of taking the gloomiest view of the future and yet going on with the job, swore that, for all their talk of peace, our lives were not worth an hour's purchase.

'When the council broke up and the Indians returned to their tepees, we sought our tents, and presently a message came from Ute chiefs that, as all was settled and now secure, Shawano himself would give us a grand display of his warriors in full array. It was noon, and I noticed that the Indian visitors who had hung about our camp disappeared. We had just eaten our midday meal, when the cry was raised, "Here they come!" and, running out, Matthews and I beheld, half a mile off, a long, long line of Indian warriors riding toward us at a gallop. Out they dashed, fully eight hundred strong, from the timber, where they had evidently been gathering, into the open park, their gleaming guns in their hands, their faces black with war paint, their naked bronze bodies shining in the bright sun, the feathers in their long hair dancing behind them in the breeze. Shawano himself in all his glory led them, his gorgeous war-bonnet of eagle plumes streaming out four feet behind him. To right, to left, he circled in swinging curves, the endless line of warriors following him; then as if by magic he sent separate bands flying this way and that, forwards and backwards, weaving a maze of figures like a dance. And every man of the eight hundred as he raced along seemed to be a part of his pony, whose swift twinkling hoofs bore him hither and thither as though man and horse were one.

'"I never saw cavalry do evolutions better," said the General, eyeing them intently, his big, burly form a yard or two in advance of them, the rest of us with Godfrey and his wife close up behind. Her lips looked drawn with the tense strain of that anxious morning, but her eyes were soft; she was remembering her baby. "How in the world does Shawano manage it, General?" asked Captain Alexander. "He doesn't shout, and he doesn't use a bugle. Yet they all know exactly what he means."

'"You've got me there," answered the General. "It's A number one; but the way he does it beats me."

'Nearer to us in the plain scoured the flying

waves of horsemen, and closer they wheeled and closer still, till we could count the stripes of paint on their faces and bodies and see each panting pony's wide red nostrils "like pits full of blood to the brim." We had been speaking in undertones before, perhaps half-awed by the spectacle. Now we all fell suddenly silent.

'What did the Indians mean? I cannot say what was in other men's minds; I only know my own, and the thought that flashed up was "Treachery." For the next instant there was a terrific yell, and the whole line of Indians came straight for us at a charge, firing their guns. Yell followed yell, and the air was filled with cracking, fire-shots, and whizzing bullets. I saw Godfrey's wife throw herself in front of him. Was it the woman's sacrifice to shield her man from the leaden hail, or to remind him to give her the merciful bullet?

'"This is the end," I thought; but the big General in front stood like a rock.

'Up, up they came, and then, at the last second, their line split apart in the middle and each half-dashed by us to right and to left, the foam-flakes from their snorting ponies floating to the ground at our feet; and then away in a cloud they dashed off into the pines to reload their empty guns. We stood unharmed.

'The babel had stopped and there was a great silence. "Just a little game to try our nerves," said the General's firm voice to Captain Alexander. "I knew they were only fooling us when I heard their bullets go high. But I want to compliment that Mr. Shawano on his skill as a cavalry leader. Won't you call him up for me, Mrs. Godfrey?" His eyes were still following the Indians, whom they had never left for a moment. Now for the first time he looked back.

'But Mrs. Godfrey did not hear him; her wonderful nerve had given away at last, and she lay in a dead faint in her husband's arms.

'"She may be only a Ute half-breed," muttered Matthews, "but she's a white woman under her skin."

'I did admire the splendid courage and coolness of the Governor in the face of that charge of eight hundred savage warriors. Had he shown a sign of flinching, it is possible that some of us who were behind might have turned tail, and then who knows? That wild charge might have become deadly earnest, and then every last one of us would have been wiped out.

'But that very evening in the Ute camp I

had a chance to see a courage and coolness dis-
played which I admired even more if possible.
The Utes gave us a scalp-dance. They had always been enemies of the Plains Indians, and
had lately gone down on the Plains for a buf-
falo hunt, and had returned triumphant; they
had got a splendid lot of robes and, what was
better than all, they had surprised some un-
lucky Cheyennes and had killed and scalped
one of their braves and captured his little six-
year-old son alive. The dance was a weird
sight; the firelight flickered on the naked,
painted bodies of the dancers and the fresh
scalp hung waving in the wind on a pole in the
center of the ring, and there, at the foot of the
pole alone in the midst of his enemies, danced
the captive child. For hours I watched that
baby; he was helpless in the hands of his cap-
tors — he was put there to dance; and he
danced; but oh, how unwilling! First one little
foot was raised a bare half-inch from the ground
and slowly set down again; then the other was
lifted the same way in its turn and as slowly
set down, dance he must, and he knew it; but
it was the most lugubrious movement imagin-
able, and all the while I watched, never once
did that child look up, either to the scalp of his
father waving over his head or to the ring of

fierce faces, the faces of the deadly enemies of his tribe, that surrounded him.

'"What will they do with him?" I asked Godfrey, who also enjoyed the privilege of looking on at the spectacle.

'"Can't say for certain," he answered. "The kid's obstinate as a pig now, but likely he'll forget his own people before long, and the Utes will adopt him into their tribe and bring him up as a Ute. Maybe you'll see him on the war-path hunting for his Cheyenne uncle's scalp before he's twenty."

'"But if he doesn't forget," I queried — "if he chooses to be a pig and remain obstinate, what, then?"

'"Oh," said Godfrey, "in that case, likely they'll tie him to a stake and torture him the next time they feel like having a circus. These Utes are bound to have a prisoner — it may be a Cheyenne or it may be another — every once in a while, to make a holy show of. It relieves their feelings. But you and I won't get no tickets for that show. They'll take darn good care to keep it a secret from the whites. Governor McCook here wouldn't stand no such performance."

'To this day I cannot tell which I would put higher, the courage of the trained soldier, the man in charge, that Governor of the Territory, or that of the helpless Cheyenne boy alone in the midst of his enemies.'

I usually rode with Primo, a born gentleman, who always waited for me to start the conversation. I tried always to talk of things that would interest him — his team mostly. For hours we would never speak. Then I would say, 'I believe I will walk for a while, Primo,' and he would stop, let me off, drive on out of sight; then, gentleman that he was, halt the horses, and wait for me to come up to him. Once, while waiting, he went into an old abandoned cabin, and found a tattered mildewed magazine. In it was a poem by Ella Wheeler Wilcox, called, I think, 'Crucifixion,' which was to the effect that we make such a fuss over crucifying Christ and yet go on doing it each day in our treatment of laboring children, animals, and other races. Also in it was a picture of Christ on the cross. I hung it on the wall of the tent, and felt that it was a sort of a protection, and I always keep it in my bedroom now.

We made camp beside the Los Pinos, just as full of fish now as when Mr. Townshend was there. One day Earl was fishing and had a line with three hooks on it. I called him and he dropped his pole for the moment. When he returned, he had three fish.

The first things we unloaded were the cook-tent and the dining-tent, the stove, and the supplies. Our tables were boards on trestles. All the tables were white-oilcloth-covered, all the dishes were white enamel. In our camp there was a place for everything, and there it was placed. Now, many years later, if we were unloading, I'm sure both the Boss and I would know where every box, dish, knife and fork, pan, and kettle should go. Our case goods were stacked on one side of the cook-tent, till it seemed almost like the shelves in a store. My opened sacks of sugar, flour, cornmeal, and so on were kept in a large mouse-fly-proof grub-box. Above my work-table, in boxes supplied with shelves, I kept lard, salt, pepper, extracts, soda, baking powder, and so on. As far as I know, I was the only one in camp who had whiskey, which was used in case of emergency and for pudding sauce. In the dining-tent were the long table and my bed, which last was always covered with a white sheet. It was a sanitary cot with folding sides. No man in all my years of camping ever sat on my bed except an underbred forest ranger, who rode up one day, and, leaving the saddle and pack on his tired horses, came in to wait for dinner. He threw himself full length, spurs and all, on my bed. And when I told him it wasn't done and suggested he feed and water his horses, he looked at me, hurt, and in an 'ain't-women-fools' manner.

Our fresh meat was brought by the quarter or half, and in the daytime was kept rolled in canvas. At night it was hung high in a tree.

At each new camp, men were set to digging a pit for a toilet; also a second pit in front of the cook-tent, into which all waste, empty cans, and wash-water was thrown. Before leaving a camp, both these pits were filled in and covered over with dirt; also all débris was burned.

In spite of the hard work, getting up before daylight, and not getting to bed before ten, I loved it all — the restfulness of running water and rustling leaves, the dancing shadows of leaves on the tent, either in sunlight or moonlight; grasses swaying in the wind, frost-painted bushes, the twitter and song of birds, the buzz of flies, the daring and triumphant whine of mosquitoes, the rasping call of blue jay and camp robber, the chirrup of chipmunks, the whistle of conies and the rustle and squeak of mice, men's voices in narrative and argument, usually laughing, seldom quarreling,

better-behaved than in their own homes — I
don't know why, except that they had most of
the home comforts and no home irritations.
Then, too, being close to nature brings out the
best in humanity. But, after all, the main
cause of their contentment was that they were
well-fed. I felt my position as providing their
muscle and morale.

Food was as carefully selected, cooked, and
decorated as though we were in an expensive
hotel. And (this is a secret) desserts, although
lots of work, are much cheaper than beans,
meat, and bread. Once, one of the men called
me a 'workin' fool,' but you see I enjoyed it.
I was expressing myself. Somewhere I have a
season's menu — more Government red tape
— and you'd be surprised to read it. This
would be a sample — Breakfast: Hot, well-
cooked cereal, a different kind each day of the
week so they would not tire; coffee; stewed
dried fruit, each day different; either bacon,
ham and eggs, or fresh fish, fried potatoes, hot
biscuits always, and either coffee cake, doughnuts, or cookies. Dinner: Soup, tea and coffee,
a meat of some kind, with gravy, potatoes,
another vegetable — if canned, cooked differently from the usual manner; hot rolls, a salad
— yes, a salad, in the mountains where there

was no lettuce, but there were canned vegetables, cabbage, potatoes, apples, and fish.
For dessert we'd have pie with hard sauce and
cheese. Supper would be much the same as
dinner, except that we would have no soup,
and have cake and pudding for dessert.

For Sundays I planned something special,
and always made lemon pie — and I make good
ones! I'd also make a huge platter of candy.

Holidays were observed by decorations on
salads or cakes. Once, on Primo's birthday, I
baked and decorated a cake for him, and when
they were all seated at the table, I took it in
and put it beside his plate. There was much
talk and shouting from every one except Primo
— he only smiled up at me — his winning
smile.

Instinctively, Mexicans are well-mannered.
When they had finished eating, Primo asked
me for a clean knife, then stood and cut his
cake, walked along the benches and passed it
to each man there, then to me. When the men
were all gone, he came to me and thanked me
for my kindness.

We had few camp rules. Of these I remember only that there was to be no swearing, no
wrestling in cook- or dining-tent, and that it
was a crime for a man to call my attention by

tapping on a cup. If a newcomer swore in cook- or dining-tent — really they both were one — the men looked at him and maybe frowned; anyway, he was made to understand he had committed a *faux pas*. I don't know how to spell or say it, but I know what it means. And no birds or chipmunks were to be killed.

One Sunday, after the dinner work was done, I climbed a near-by mountain. I wanted to be alone. The men were doing their Sunday cleaning-up, washing their clothes, cutting hair, shaving, and so on. After a time I heard the crack of guns, and thought they were shooting at a mark, but when I returned, in the pit I saw, sticking out from loose new dirt, the tips of bushy tails, and the gray and blue of jay and camp-robber wings. I didn't say anything (out loud), but for two Sundays they had no candy.

Many times we could have had venison, but the Boss would not allow it; he thought that a Government camp should be mighty particular in regard to the law. The wildest meat we ever had was groundhog, which I cooked to please the Boss's brother. When skinned, groundhogs look like cats and smell to high heaven, worse than skunks, because, whatever may be said of a skunk, it is not a dirty smell.

This was. I soaked it in soda water, filled it with onion dressing, getting madder as I worked, and every time the oven door was opened, the smell was louder. By supper-time I was actually sick. As I remember, the brother was the only one who ate any, and he pretended to like it.

Constructing a telephone line is like doing many other things, there's much more to it than you'd think. From the choosing of timber, which has to have the forest ranger's 'U.S.' stamped in it, to the cutting, trimming, skidding, snaking and hauling, and getting the first message over the line, it is hard, interesting work. There was the surveying, and then the digging of the holes; each hole had to come up to specifications — so many feet deep, so many inches around and apart. Often they were sunk with the aid of dynamite, into solid rock. The creosoting followed; each pole was swung upright — three at a time, I think — into a tank of boiling creosote. Everything was done by rule, until the creosote penetrated the wood just so far. I disliked this part of the work most of all — the fumes from hot tanks filling the air, men with burned bodies, eyes, faces, and hands. Wherever the creosote spattered, it took both skin and clothes. Then there were yellow stains all over the dishes, tables, and towels.

Next, I think, came the putting on of the cross-arms, braces, pegs, and transformers; then the setting of the poles, plumbed and measured to specifications; and the stringing of the wire. Oh, the satisfaction of being able to call Central and to feel we were homeward bound! (I am just remembering all this, which would, I expect, make the Boss smile.) We followed the line as it was finished and moved camp every two or three weeks.

After our second move, the supervisor, his family, and some of the head men from Denver visited us. Neita came with them. While they were with us, there was a dance at the ranger station, six or eight miles down the canyon. Most of the men, including the 'main squeeze,' as the men called him, and Neita and I decided to go. I left the supper dishes and Earl, crying at the top of his voice because he couldn't go along. My good sister-in-law did the dishes.

It was dark when we left and sprinkling rain. Soon it was very dark and the road could be seen only by the flashes of lightning, but we had a wonderful teamster and finally arrived very damp, except as to spirits. I always have a good time. That night I had an especially good one. We danced and sang and ate and danced again. I understood the Denver man was a writer; if so, that night for him was full of local color. I should really like to read his version of it. I should also like to know just what he was thinking the night that I glanced up from picking over next day's beans and caught his eye fastened on me with such a queer, penetrating look. In my life there have been so many 'ships that pass in the night' without ever 'hailing each other in passing.'

Many people, after reading 'The Life of an Ordinary Woman,' feel sorry for me. I wish they wouldn't. I am really the happiest person I've ever met. I've had a full, rich life which I'd not exchange for a safer, more stupid one.

Late that fall, when we finished, I went home with enough money to pay the bank the one hundred dollars I had borrowed when Neita graduated from high school. In our town much is made over commencement — gifts, parties, and, of course, clothes; and there must be no difference between the well-to-do man's child and mine. Foolish? I don't think so. Pride? No! — Well, maybe so; but I just didn't want my child hurt as I, when a child, and later — was hurt.

There was enough left, after paying for this, to have some much-needed dentistry done and to ensure our winter's coal and wood. Neita, that winter did not return to college. Instead, she became engaged, and the following spring was married.

At this time there was war in Europe, but our own personal affairs were closer at hand and so much more important that we paid little attention to it.

I spread myself on Neita's wedding; it was to be a real affair. She had lovely clothes, all made by me even to the blue silk going-away suit. I planned, and cooked, and decorated with the wild flowers that Jose brought from Bonanza. It was a lovely wedding. After luncheon for about twenty guests, she and Jack — I haven't told you about Jack; he was a teacher in the high school and was and is a fine, good man whom I am glad and proud to have for a son-in-law — left for Jack's home in Ohio. And I even sent wedding announcements — announcements that you were perfectly free to run your fingers over; and somehow, in mailing them, the one to a prominent family, who had given her lovely silver, was lost. There was a 'to-do' over it — when one gets out of one's groove the way is beset with dangers.

I hadn't expected to miss Neita the way I did miss her, and as the days passed I realized what Browning meant when he said something like this: 'We rear them and we love them, then we lose them.'

CHAPTER V

I, who fall short in managing my own affairs, can see just how it would profit my neighbor if I managed his.

A. E.

THAT year I was sort of down in the mouth, so I was glad when the Government work started again. We had almost all of our former gang and a few new ones. Of course, the greatest among us, was Jumbo, with new polished harness which had brighter, brassier knobs than ever. Every man on the job, I think, hated, feared, and admired him. On this trip he performed beautifully, although loaded as no self-respecting mule should be loaded. When after a hard day's drive, we were a few miles from our destination, making road as we went, the men cutting trees (this always hurt me), and throwing rocks and fallen timber to one side, then, in one of these bad places, Jumbo quit on us. He used the greatest judgment, for to have this heavy wagon back down the grade meant disaster. Every one was out blocking wheels; then all hands, except the cook, took turns, whipping and beating Jumbo, who would lunge and kick every direction — except forward; sometimes jumping onto and over his

[67]

team mate, who stood patiently, meek and trembling, ready to throw himself into the harness at the first move Jumbo would make to pull. I don't remember this one's name — mules are like men, the good meek ones leave small impress on our minds. When Jumbo staged one of his tantrums, I used to get out of reach and out of sight if I could, straining every nerve and muscle, saying to myself, 'Oh, Jumbo, do go on! Oh, please, Jumbo, I can't stand this beating! Oh, Jumbo, this time move — move!' — while another part of me said, 'Don't give in, Jumbo! Your load is too heavy, and you know it. To think of them, beating you so — the fools! Don't let them break you, Jumbo, don't!'

Once I simply could not stand it, and crying and holding my hands over my eyes, I ran through the timber, thinking of the blood and the broken ears of Jumbo. I cried aloud, 'I can't stand it — I just can't!' I ran a mile or more when I heard the sound of wheels behind me. The Boss had sent Bill on with the spring wagon to pick me up. I refused, and trudged on. Bill, on his part, was pouting, too — old men are like old tom cats, they get sensitive, sullen, and cranky; besides, he was doing what he had been sent to do. If I did not want to get in, it wasn't up to him to coax me. So on we went. When I walked fast, he drove fast; when I went slowly, he stopped the team and sat like a humped-up idol, signifying, 'I speak not — see not — hear not.'

This finally got the best of my sense of humor, and I laughed and climbed in. He had in the wagon the makings for supper. The Boss had an eye and a stomach to the future, even though he was trying to move that immovable object, a determined and stationary mule.

We drove on silently; usually I took the lead in conversations, trying to draw these men out. That day I was too hurt. There, on top of the high mountains, it was beautiful. Trees crowded the old road so that we could hardly weave through them, and the wheels sank into the deep pine needles; there was, too, the glint of slender blue columbines, making me catch my breath, till, after a while, I was soothed.

Then we came to Cathedral, where we were to camp. There was a cow camp here and I went in and started preparations for supper, the cowboy helping. He had fresh veal — so he said; but I suspected it was 'whisper meat,' as Ellis, a young niece of mine, calls venison. He cut enough for our gang, and I made hot corn bread and prepared an extra good supper (nothing like it to soothe ruffled feelings), then waited — and waited. It was late and raining. The cowboy urged me to go to bed, offering to keep supper warm for our crew. Finally I went to bed in an extra bed some cowboy had left. It was cleaner than one would expect. I put a clean dish towel over the pillow. Before I dropped asleep, I heard them coming through the driving rain.

Some of the weak sisters rushed for warmth and shelter; others, led by the Boss, who was the first and the last to leave any job, unhitched and unloaded. I overheard 'Christ-a-mighty, there's a bed-roll fell in the creek'; then, disgustedly, 'Hell of a lot of difference whether it's in the creek or wagon, they're all soaked.'

I knew it was my bed. It was. So ended that day.

The next morning there was no joking among us; getting breakfast was a very business-like performance. We were polite to each other, choosing our language carefully. They all called me Mrs. Ellis. A good dinner seemed to loosen things up somewhat, and after an extra good supper, we were almost back on our old footing.

Where we were then, I think is one of the

most beautiful places in this country of beauty.
Just back of us was the high cathedral rock,
every pink granite spire, abutment, and tower
standing as though intentionally designed and
placed by a master hand. I expect it was too.
Looking up the stream, one saw the high bare
peaks in front of Creede. Before us were tow-
ering, deeply wooded mountains — the pine
trees coming down to the water's edge; below
us the rugged cliffs, where the stream emptied
into the swift, tumbling Cebolla, which, pro-
nounced 'Se-voya,' is Mexican, and means
'onion.'

The next day we moved on. They did not
arrange for me to go with the main gang. Bill
and I were to follow, waiting for the tents to be
pitched. Besides, I suppose they just didn't
want me, although by now they had a driver
who could manage Jumbo: it was Slim, who had
turned his own mules over to another driver.
I never knew what Slim did, and don't want to
either, but I think he unharnessed Jumbo and
beat him with the trace chains until he con-
quered him; at least, after that, when Jumbo
showed signs of balking, Slim had only
to rattle the trace chains to have Jumbo
lunge forward into the harness. And how he
could pull when he wanted to! Jumbo was

really one of the finest individuals I've ever known.

Bill and I had the men's suitcases on our load and when we were fording the swollen stream, one of them dropped off. In an instant Bill was out in the water up to his knees, fishing that suitcase from the river. As usual, it was raining. I had on a heavy coat and what we then called a peach-basket hat; it was once trimmed with hanging bunches of cherries and was quite shapely. It shed rain, and had been in so many storms that by now it was stretched till it covered my shoulders. Bill had on only his work clothes — no coat and thin overalls. I took part of my coat and spread it over his wet, trembling knees. With the back of one hand he wiped the rain off his dripping nose and with the other threw the coat back over me. Again I spread it over his lap and snuggled up close, so that it would cover both of us, and said, 'Don't be foolish.' This broke the chill of the last two days. Once more we were friends, and as we drove through the pouring rain, he told me of the wonderful doughnuts his wife could make (they had been divorced for years and he always spoke of her with the greatest love and respect). 'Better than yours, but I will give you credit for making the best corn bread a man ever flopped his lip over.'

I remembered, and always after this cut the crustiest, brownest piece and placed it on his plate, which was — although I didn't then know it — casting bread upon the waters.

The Cebolla fish — I don't know why — are the finest, fattest, firmest trout I've ever cooked or eaten. There was a washtub full all the time waiting to be cooked. (Bill and Primo were our best fishermen.) We had them every meal, and the more you ate, the better they were. For breakfast I would fry several panfuls, laying them in closely, head to tail; then, when they were well browned, I slipped a knife under the fish, my outspread hand over them, and quickly turned them all at once. I became so expert that with almost one motion I could slip my hand down a fish, removing the water; then salt and pepper it inside and out, roll it in cornmeal, then slip it into the pan. The largest were baked and served with different sauces. When cold, they were picked from the bones, made into salad, or creamed, escalloped, or used in croquettes; and, in spite of all this supposedly mental provender, our brains seemed no better.

In a group of men there are always a few

loyal good workers, some average, and a slacker or two — usually one agitator, who is lazy, and influences far better men than himself, and by suggestion gets them to lie down on the job. We had one. He grew tired, and did every possible thing to be fired, but could not make a go of it. The Boss said, 'By God, I'll never pay his transportation home. He'll either stick, or walk out.' He stuck; although the day he said, when I sent canned salmon for lunch after we had been having trout twice a day for weeks, 'If this keeps up we'll all sprout fins,' I thought it clever, but the Boss, who overheard him, thought otherwise, and almost fired him.

But in spite of everything the line went on — so did the cook. Of course, we had our tense times; for instance, I was frying potatoes, stirring and turning them with one of my butcher knives, which, to a man is like a red rag to a bull. The Boss stood it as long as he could; then, 'Sis, don't you know better than to stir potatoes with the butcher knife?' I was tired; besides, I've heard men harp on this before — 'I like to stir potatoes this way.' He was disgusted and said, 'It's past me why no woman has any sense when it comes to tools.' Then, to me, in a teaching tone,

'Don't you know it takes the temper out of them?' I jabbed the knife harder — 'Well, what of it?' Now, if the knife was losing temper, I was gaining it, and said, 'You make me tired! Don't you ever say butcher knife to me again. You men, who have a new lay-out of tools every job, expect me to use the same seventy-five-cent butcher knife year after year, when I'll bet the picks, shovels, and crowbars you've broken and lost would fill a wagon-bed.' He gave me a 'There's-no-use' look and left; later I heard him say, 'Cook's on the prod.'

I was always tired — so tired that at night I would lie awake, fearing, worrying, and knowing that if I did not sleep, I should not be able to do the next day's work; so tired that many times, when the men were all down at the table eating, between pouring their first and second cup of coffee, I would go outside the tent, and throw myself full length on the ground, face to the sky, and, with one ear turned to the infinite and the other to the eating men, I absorbed strength.

I remember, one night in particular, after cooking all day for fourteen men, I had finished my supper dishes (often the Boss or another wiped them for me) and had set the sponge for the next day's baking — it always had to be wrapped and wrapped to keep it warm. I had sliced the ham and had put it to freshen, then had put the oatmeal or cracked wheat to soak, and had covered everything carefully to keep the mice out. It was nine o'clock, and I blew out the candle and washed in the dark. It was a beautiful moonlight night with the shadows of trees dancing on the tent. I pulled a box in front of the stove and pushed away the kindling left there to dry, lifted my swollen feet to the oven door, and looked in at the glowing coals — and hurt. I was one ache inside and out — inside, the worst. 'Is this all I'm ever to know of life? And if it is, why must I feel?' There was a rustle at the tent-flap — 'Are you in bed, Annie? I want — a drink before turning in.' I hastily pulled my clothes together, but did not move. I was too sunk. A man reached in, untied the tent, came to where I was sitting, and laid his hand on my shoulder. It took all my strength to shrug it off, and say, 'Get your drink, and go.' He drank, pouring as we always did, part on the ground — a sort of a libation, I suppose.

Then, wistfully, 'It's a wonderful night —

shan't I sit awhile, and we'll talk of love.'
'Love?' and I laughed, when I wanted to put
my head on his shoulder — any shoulder — and
weep my heart out. 'Love? — you make me
laugh!' And need I have added this? — it
was to keep myself in line — 'Go on to bed and
sleep — then maybe tomorrow you can dig
your allotment of holes.'

On a certain morning I was more happy than
usual — no need to whistle up my courage by
saying, 'This day will bring some lovely
thing'; or, 'Oh, the world is so full of a number of things, we all should be as happy as
kings'; or, 'Life is real, life is earnest, and the
grave is not its goal'; or, 'Let us, then, be up
and doing, with a heart for any fate; still
achieving, still pursuing, learn to labor and to
wait.'

That day the men had taken their lunch, and
I was alone. I heard a shout — it was a sheep-
man going to his camp on the high range. He
had brought our mail tied on the back of his
saddle. It was water-soaked from a recent
rain. When he had gone, after eating a piece
of mince pie I had handed up to him, I opened
a letter from my sister Jose and tried to read it.
It was so blurred I could only make this much
out — but that was too much: It was that the

boy and man whom I had loved and dreamed of ever since I was a little girl — was dead; he had died in Peru, unmarried. Never after were my dreams so clear — a man is the motif of all women's dreams, and, I imagine, most women do dream. That day I had a round or two with myself, and by the time the men had returned from work, supper was ready and none of them ever suspected that, a few hours before, I had buried my love and my hopes and that my dreams and castles in Spain were shattered.

So the weeks passed. We had only nine miles to the ranger station on the upper Cebolla which would be the end of our line. But, the canyon was so narrow, rocky, and rugged that it was impossible to get the wagons and equipment through; so we were compelled to go around by Lake City — a ninety-mile trip of four days.

Several of the men were sent through the canyon, the teamsters, the Boss and I going around. We were to travel through Gunnison, Lake, Mineral, and Rio Grande Counties before again reaching our own Saguache County.

For this trip I cooked days ahead — bread, cookies, doughnuts, and boiled hams, and so on. The other things would be cooked over a camp-fire. I have cooked over a camp-fire for ten or twelve men when the wind was blowing so hard that two men had to be delegated to stand and hold a wagon sheet to break the wind in order to keep the fire together and on the ground.

Have you ever ridden, in auto or train, by one of these parties of camping workmen and wondered what they were interested in and what they talked about while they squatted around their camp-fire? You'd be surprised; very little of the day's work done or to come is mentioned; very little of personal interests or affairs. A woman who once visited our camp afterward wrote me, 'Then the talks at night with the Boss, and Bill, and Royce — the influence of electricity on religious thought or some such simple subject, introduced by the boss, and he was more up on the technical details of the war than we were by far.'

They talked of the latest sporting event — especially so if it was a prize-fight, each one giving his opinion — each one, that is, except the Mexicans; they were usually quiet, but if asked, 'What do you say, Primo?' 'I read in paper two months ago he good man.' Or they talked of religion; very strong opinions about the latest in politics, crime, dress, and — yes

— society. They argued and laid bets on a tennis game and, the chances were, they had never seen one (neither had I), often calling on me as referee, 'I'll leave it to cook, I'll leave it to cook'; and — to play safe — I usually changed the subject. 'Are you riding at the Fair this fall, John?' 'Not on your life,' he answered. 'Last year when I just crawled off Hell-for-breakfast, addled, blinded, and with all my teeth jarred loose, I heard a guy say, "To do that must take a strong back and a weak head." So I'm off it.' We talked of different makes and merits of cars — none of us owned one, but you will find this is the sort of a person who knows all the ins and outs as to cars.

The first night we camped on the Cebolla, just below Cathedral. A few years later, a rich, cultured, educated, Eastern woman from Boston, a descendant of the Adams family, married a cowboy and lived at Cathedral. It would be lovely in the summers, but how did she stand it in the winters? Once I saw her — a small, poorly dressed woman with a lovely voice and manners, and (I heard) a twenty-five-thousand-dollar necklace of pearls which she wore under her clothes. The night of our first camp the men made their beds under the wagons. They did not take time to pitch the tents, but offered to pitch mine; however, I said, 'No, I like to sleep under the stars.' So my cot was set up in the open. It was wonderful to go to sleep watching the stars, to hear the men's low talk coming from their beds, the crunch and grunt of the horses and the mules, to see the dying camp-fire, snapping and flickering, not a cloud in the sky — my soul — which it very seldom was — at rest.

Then in the night I was awakened by a cloudburst — concentrated, I know, on my cot. At once myself, my long thick hair, my quilts, the pillow and the mattress beneath, were soaked; the rain still coming down in torrents. I screamed. The horses were running, the men up and after them. The Boss ran to me and threw a horse blanket over me, head and all. Under this — the horse smell choking me — I huddled in torture the long hours through till morning, when, in spite of the rain, we got a fire started. Have I forgotten, or did some one hold an umbrella while this was being done? Anyway, we dressed in wet clothes, my wet hair was twisted, and I got some kind of a breakfast. Then we broke camp, rolling the beds wet, and were on our way down and along the Cebolla — a most beautiful country.

After a while the sun came out and dried, warmed, and cheered us. To me it was a lovely trip, riding always at a walk; giving one ample time to enjoy each new beauty of sky, rock, river, tree, and flower. For this day I was especially glad because of the wild raspberries hanging red and ripe from the bushes on the banks of the road. The men were singing as we came into Powderhorn — a settlement of prosperous, kindly people, all descended from a pioneer, who with seven daughters had settled many years ago in this out-of-the-way place.

We made camp, hung the wet bedding to dry, and had supper. We discovered that there was to be a dance that night in Powderhorn. Several decided to go, I among them. I dried my hair, dressed it, and hunted out of my suitcase a lavender ratiné dress (rather damp), and pinned on a bunch of rose berries and autumn leaves.

We did not stay long at the dance; we were too tired. Long enough, however, for me to have all the men 'knocked down,' or 'made used to me.' That was their form of introduction. We were up and on the next morning — I wild with hay fever. My eyes were swollen shut. On Slim's wagon I lay curled up on

the rolls of bedding, my arm around the blacksmith forge to keep from being thrown off the
lurching load. There, crying and sneezing,
with the dust rolling up into my itching eyes,
the rank odor of sunflowers and skunkweed
beside the road choking me, I put in the day.
That night when I started toward the grub-
boxes, Boss said, 'You're all in, Sis. We'll do
it.' And he and one of the men pitched my
tent, unrolled my bed, and made it for me, and
I turned in. In the night the mules broke away,
and I saw this same faithful teamster go down
the road tracking them by the light of a lan-
tern. And I thought he stood about the same
chance of finding them as if he were Diogenes
looking for an honest man. But, by sunup,
mules and man were again on the job.

We loaded and started; going through Lake
City we stopped at the main store to get some
needed supplies. And this was the first time
that I realized that I was doing anything unusual; although, if it had been any one else, I
should have considered it so. This is probably
the way the gossip went — I know, because
at one time it's just the way I should have
talked had I been living in that mining camp:

'There's a lot of campers down by the
river.' 'Yeh, so I heard — Government con-

struction gang, building a telephone line on Cebolla — a hard lot, I'll bet, mostly Mexicans. Oh, well, the saloons will get some trade.' 'Yes; they say there's a woman among them. She must be mighty tough. No wonder men lose their respect for women. Well, all I got to say is, I've always tried to do what was right.'

I climbed off the wagon and went along with the men into the store. It was an adventure after being in the mountains so long. Shortly most of the men left on other business bent — only Primo and I were left. Then, some women came in. I glanced eagerly up and smiled. I was hungry for the sight of a woman and woman's clothes. They turned coldly away. I was crushed, and I burned with embarrassment. Primo, who never spoke to me unless spoken to first, never seeming to understand me — especially when I was prying into Mexican customs and ways — sensed my hurt, as a loving child or a faithful dog would have done, and came to me, his big soft eyes shiny with understanding and pity. He sat beside me smiling in his winning way and entertained me by making fun of the people coming into the store, taking sly digs at their manners and dress. He bought candy in a striped sack and laid it in my lap, and then —

this was the supreme sacrifice: 'My mother ees boss — she no let us spik English at home. She no let me play fiddle three years after my grandmother die. She say it's no good luck.'

Then the Boss boomed in. 'What are you and Primo doing — plotting against the whites?' Then our gang went on — on up the Slumgullion.

CHAPTER VI

Usually Pride masquerades as a Virtue, when it's only Vanity — a by-product of Selfishness.

A. E.

Now, if you are looking for scenic beauty, go over this road from Lake City to Creede. The miles, instead of being end to end, are on top of each other — which did not appeal to us, having to move heavy camp equipment up it, all of us praying that Jumbo would behave himself. After a few miles it was necessary to unhitch and double up on each wagon. We all walked, and for a while I stayed with these men and teams, fighting for almost every foot of the way. Straining, sweating mules and horses, swearing, sweating men with their shoulders to the wheels, digging their toes into the ground and pushing from behind. I walked, or, I should say, climbed on ahead. Often I rested and looked back at the steep, very high mountains rising straight up from Lake City. They were covered with mining dumps, and the shaft houses perched up there looked like sparrows' nests. Roads zigzagged in impossible-looking places. At the foot was Lake City, the cleanest mining town I've ever seen, with its substantial log houses having yards full of growing grass and flowers; and — something I appreciated very much going into or leaving a town — one saw no unsightly dump piles of old tin cans.

For hours we climbed. On every new rise I thought, 'This must be the last one.' We were on an old, old road. In the early days, stage-coaches had climbed and rattled over it. There are many tales of hold-ups and hold-up men. This was the road over which, years before, Susan B. Anthony and Elizabeth Cady Stanton had ridden horseback, taking to these booming mining camps the new idea of women's rights.

As we climbed, the trees became more scattering, dwarfed, and misshapen. After a while they were only gray skeletons of trees with bare wind-blown limbs all growing the same way. Soon we were above timberline — then, we gained the top. Oh! the lovely meadows above timberline — the ground covered with grasses and flowers, mostly the blue, pink, lavender, and white, sweet-smelling edelweiss. There is something about these high altitudes that is very peaceful and quieting. Just then we were all in need of it and dropped down upon the ground, gathering strength from it for body and mind. There we let our souls rest.

As we went on, we were quieter, more tranquil, I expect most of us wondering as I was — why all this late struggle, upheaval, and imitation — 'all's right with the world.'

Before long we heard voices, then laughter and yells, from the men who had been sent through the canyon, and they were coming to meet us. They were young and thoughtless, almost boys. Instead of making a holiday of our coming, it would have been better to have fixed the road, which was very bad. Soon we were all off; men cutting trees, promising Jumbo to kill him, if he balked; men grading the road, lifting and heaving on wheels, pushing and pulling on rocks — and the old struggle was again on, harder to bear now, as it was getting dark and soon it was raining. We went on and on. I had given up, and, as I stumbled along, slipping on the wet rocks, I was, for me, miserable.

When we finally came to camp, there was no light, no fire, and no dry wood. The boys had hunted and fished all day, and I think expected me, after this four-day trip, to come in smiling, with a hot meal all ready for them. The Boss snapped orders through the rain, emphasizing each one with oaths. Usually I hate swearing. That night it had my utmost approval. I slumped down upon a box, wet and miserable, thinking if I was to die for it, that this was one night when I couldn't get supper. I was ashamed, too, at not being able to do my part.

Soon there was a fire going; always, when there was no dry wood at hand, they would knock a piece off of that old Government truck — Jumbo and I were glad. My tent was up. The Boss came to me, saying, 'Well, Sis, what's it going to be?' I did not then know, but he has since told me, that I was crying, and I gasped through my sobs, 'To-to-ma-to soup, I guess.' Then this man — and he is a man — with the help of faithful Primo and Slim, who had by now attended to their teams (since daylight each of these men had been straining every nerve and muscle of brain and body), hunted out two big stew kettles and poured condensed milk into one and several cans of tomatoes into the other. When piping hot, they combined the two, then called to the men, 'Come and get it.' I heard the Boss say, 'A little less noise, fellows; cook's all in.' Then at the tent-flap, 'Sis, here's something to warm the cockles of your heart'; and he handed me hot soup and coffee. It did, and I slept, slept my first night in this camp in which something was to happen that, years later, would be the turning-point in my life.

Many times the men took their lunch and would be gone all day. Those days were the greatest pleasure to me. I could cook and commune, with only the birds and the chipmunks to break the silence. On days like those only my busy body was in the tent; my mind and thoughts were all in my newly built castles in Spain. By the time the dishes were done, I was sailing the seven seas; during the baking of the bread, the cakes, and the pies, I was in Paris buying clothes; I was there, too, when sweeping the floors, which were hard-packed ground often sprinkled to keep the dust down, full of many hills and hollows worn by my countless steps; while washing the towels and tea-towels which was, for me, a back-breaking job and needed strong treatment; while my hands were crushing those creosote-stained and dirt-begrimed towels up and down the washboard, I was trailing silken garments down a marble stairway. As I paused at the bottom, my beautiful hand resting on the newel post, I was met by a man — a man with laughter wrinkles in the corners of his eyes. He took my hand and we passed through a carved door — then — I hung the towels over the guy ropes. No, not snow-white; but maybe the sun and wind will bleach them.

It was always afternoon before I was through. Then, after fixing fresh flowers for the dining-table, I washed, combed my hair, and changed my dress. Every day I changed into fresh clean clothes — it rested my soul and body. It was very seldom I was without a bunch of flowers or leaves pinned high on one shoulder. This strengthened me.

One such dreaming day, after doing all that was to be done, I tied the tent-flaps together, as it was blowing and sprinkling rain. I sat down to rest, tired now of my own dreams and fancies; as the body tires, then is the time to live in the dreams of another. That day it was with Shakespeare. I was lost in 'Hamlet,' when I was startled by a woman's voice — a cultivated voice. The tent-flaps were pulled open and she asked me if she and her husband might stay with us. Quickly I untied the inside strings and let her in, and we sized up each other. I saw money — this, while it is not the first thing I look for, is, I'm sorry to say, the first thing I notice; then

I found breeding, beauty, and strength. She saw a tall, slender blue-eyed woman with a large braid of blonde hair twisted around her head, and with small, well-shaped hands and feet. Recently a woman said to me, by way of compliment, 'One can see by your hands that you have never done any hard work.' I did not explain, because she was one who could never have understood, one who pays for brainless work and kicks because she gets it. My visitor was dressed in a coat reaching below the knee and in high boots and pants, while I was traveling over the dirt floor in a dress below my shoe-tops. Then Mr. Armstrong, my guest's husband, came in; an intelligent, handsome, kindly man. I wonder why it is that the more people mean to us and the more we think of them, the harder they are to describe. It is so with the Armstrongs. At once I set out a meal for them. I found they were wealthy Chicago people, taking their vacation by riding from one old mining camp to another.

On this trip they were going from Creede to Lake City and had lost their way, and had met one of our teamsters going to Creede for grain; he had told them of our camp. Mrs. Armstrong had hesitated — naturally, I suppose; and Slim, sensing this hesitation, said,

'But there is a lady cook.' They stayed with us three days, and I enjoyed every minute of it — having some one to talk to and praise my cooking. I did my best, and, as it has since proved, was casting the Government grub on the waters which after many years returned to me in the very bread of life.

We remained in this camp till late fall. Each day bands of sheep brought from the high range passed our place; each night there was heavy frost and thick ice on the stream running by the tent. The day before we broke camp, the tents were weighted with snow. We were all glad to be starting home — all except the trouble-maker, a weak, lazy, big-mouthed liar, thinking there was no honor among men, no virtue among women, and that every woman was willing and waiting for the right man, and that he was the man.

The first day out he declared he wouldn't lift his hand to work on the way home. The Boss overheard him (deaf as he was) and at lunch ordered him to set the table — a wagon sheet spread on the ground. The trouble-maker took the plates, stood off, and tossed them at the sheet. The Boss called him down, and there was that tension in the air that almost hurts. Then the Boss ordered him to drive Slim's mules — Slim had Jumbo. 'By God,' the Boss said, 'I'll show him!' At supper there were mutterings. The trouble-maker got up and went into the timber. Slim got up and followed. I knew they were going to fight it out and, much as I would have liked to see the trouble-maker beaten up and much as he needed it, still, I couldn't stand it, and I asked the Boss to go and settle both of them. He went — the rest of the men looked at me rather resentfully. I don't know what was said or done, but from then on, we had peace. We went home by Creede and Del Norte, and then we were once more in Saguache.

The following spring Neita was to be a mother and wanted me to come; I wanted to go, and did. It was my first time to go East. I stayed until Marjorie Anne was one month old, then I started again for Colorado. On that same day we went into war and at once I saw signs of it. Every bridge was guarded; in the railroad yards men were drilling. In Chicago I saw a trainload of young men, almost boys, starting for training camps; such a seemingly happy, yelling mob overflowing the cars. And I envied them. At first I did not think much about the war. I had sense enough not

to believe all of the stories I heard; I didn't
think such things could be. Then Irvin Cobb
went overseas and wrote of it in such a manner
that one was led to believe that unheard-of,
dreadful things were really happening. Then
I went to war, or tried to. I wrote to any and
every one who I thought might get me into a
canteen or overseas, or anything just to go.
One day I received a letter from Washington
telling me there were many women just as
anxious to go as I was, and, as they lived
nearer New York, they would be sent. I
was disappointed, and as Earl and I walked up
the street, I tore the letter to bits and threw
them into the ditch. Earl, who also was frantic to go over, said, 'I'm glad of it — it serves
you right! It's all your fault, anyway; if you'd
"borned" me sooner, I could have gone.'

I borrowed money from the bank and bought
one of the first Liberty Bonds sold in Saguache; and I saved tinfoil and peachstones
(what for, I wonder?), and sugar. To have
sugar doled out was no hardship to me, because I had very seldom bought over fifty
cents' worth at one time.

I remember once, years before, I was on the
election board, and on the table before us was
a cigar-box with a slit cut in the top. This

was a graft, and people, especially candidates, were supposed and urged to drop change into the box to be used later to treat the hardworking (?) board. This time I speak of I was the only woman on the board, and the men suggested that I take the spoils — a matter of seven dollars. I did and bought with it a sack of sugar; then at night I lay awake, fearing the house would burn. Verily, affluence brings anxiety!

How suspicious we were during the war! Two men wanted to rent my house. They did not think it necessary to tell me their family history, only said they must have seclusion and quiet. I wouldn't rent it to them; I *knew* they were bomb-makers, when now, I expect, they were only bootleggers or — maybe — writers.

One night after supper, Earl and I had pains in our midriff; we knew it was pounded glass in the fig cookies we had eaten because, didn't somebody's cousin know a man who had heard that there was danger in factory products? Gosh, what fools! I was even hurt when Jeannette Rankin, the Montana Congresswoman, cried and said, 'I can't vote for war.' Now we see that she was brave and right and had vision.

I sewed at home all the time and was tired, but every day I went to the Red Cross rooms and cut out garments — thousands of garments. The women, all in their big white aprons and with the white caps around their heads, looked beautiful, and we sewed and made bandages. I never got beyond the eye-wipe bandage. I wonder if those thousands of triangular monstrosities were ever used for anything? And we knitted — I mean the others knitted — and I made one sweater. It started pretty well, but as it went on, it spread down and out and was finished with a ripple and a point. I am glad not to know the contempt and curses of the doughboy who received it.

The war did not touch me closely, as none of my friends or relatives were there. Still, I will not say that, because Jumbo, the Government mule, was there. And somehow I like to think of Jumbo being there — he in his line was so competent, so efficient; and I like to think that in some wild, stirring battle that Jumbo's brave soul passed.

All my life I had wanted to pray, and, not liking the usual prayers, I had a homemade, workable set. But during the war even those would not work. Besides, I was afraid to pray, because, of course, it would be for us to win;

that we might be the stronger in this butchering, this killing and maiming of men — men whose own women were praying just as hard that they might be the best butchers. I prayed to God to stop it; He didn't. Then I thought, some great good will come from it; it hasn't. I can't pray any more.

CHAPTER VII

I do not like the way the cards are shuffled,
But still, I like the game and want to play;
And through the long, long night will I, unruffled,
Play what I get, until the break of day.
EUGENE F. WARE: 'Whist'

I WAS tired and lonely and decided to go East
and live near Neita. A short time after my
arrival in Ohio, I met a husband and wife.
She was a neurotic woman, who completely
ruled her strong, uncomplaining husband.
After I knew them, I often wished that, instead of being kind, he would kick her. I,
because they heard I was cheerful, had the
chance of going to Ann Arbor with them as a
companion. They paid my fare and I was to
get six dollars per week. I found that in ad-
dition to being cheerful and entertaining, I
must do the cooking, cleaning, mending, and
housework for six; and during the three months
that I was there, I never did one thing right.
For three months I carried her breakfast upstairs to her bed — yes, cheerfully; and there
was not one time but the toast was too pale
or too brown, the bacon too crisp or not crisp
enough, the coffee too weak or not weak enough.

[99]

In those three months I never got time to read, and was starved for it. There were no days nor hours off. The only way I could stand it was, in the evening, to go to town — a long walk through the snow. I always passed first through the arch in the Engineers' Building and on through the University grounds. There I saw my first flag filled with gold stars, and I thought they were beautiful until I knew what they stood for. One night, I went to something in a fine building on the campus, and at every doorway there were barrels into which the crowd — many knitting women — threw hundreds of cigarettes — all kinds and brands — for the boys 'somewhere in France.'

I managed to stand it till Thanksgiving; then, when I bought a bunch of carnations to grace the dinner table, and my employer called me down for so recklessly and foolishly spending my money, I almost quit — but didn't. Soldiers were drilling on the campus. Every one was war-working, and I wanted to help. So I made arrangements to go at seven in the evening and work until ten; but when my employer, who was — she thought — too sick to work, heard of this, she objected unless she got the badge or whatever it was, and the credit for my work.

Then at Christmas, she bought several things that she wanted, and a small gift for each of the rest, excepting the patient husband. Instead, for him, she hung on the tree a note, saying that after the holidays, when the stores were having their sales, a necktie would be purchased for him. She signed it — 'Santa Claus.'

On New Year's Day, I left in the worst blizzard I've ever seen. The taxi could hardly get to the station; the train waited hours trying to pull out. It finally did go several yards, then backed up. Every one got off and sat all day in the station; the storm was so bad that no one could venture forth for food.

Along in the afternoon two men bundled up to the eyes and fought their way to a restaurant and returned with sandwiches. Everything was at a standstill, with no taxis or streetcars moving. We saw we were there for the night, and one or two others and I wrapped in everything we had and started uptown; we couldn't see or breathe or speak; we went forward with bent heads for a few steps, then turned, and backed up until we could get our breath and bearings. We were blown down and rolled over, and when we came to a doorway we leaned in its shelter and rested. At last, exhausted, trembling, and tasting blood from our raw throats and pounding hearts, we made the Y.W.C.A. and went supperless to bed.

Next day the snow-encrusted train left, and I went to Wilmington, to find the family were almost living in the bathroom, as coal was being doled out by the bucketful, and potatoes were more than a luxury. There I picked up Earl and we were off for Colorado and the San Luis Valley. In Cincinnati, when I was buying our tickets, I almost fainted when the clerk told me the price — fifteen dollars more than I had. So we put our heads together and figured. By sitting up all the way and by not eating often nor much, we made it.

We had several hours to wait before the train left. There were two cheap ways of entertainment open to us. We could not sit in the station, because it was flooded. Another was to go to the river and see a huge boat which was caught in an ice jam. This would have cost nothing, and I was for it. Earl wanted to visit the Zoo, which would cost the street-car fare; Earl won. We started for the Zoo and rode for hours, straight up a hill, and arrived just as the gates were being closed for the evening.

Home never seemed so good to me. Somehow we Westerners don't take life or ourselves as seriously as Easterners do. Then, with a promise from Neita and Jack that they, too, would soon be on their way toward Colorado, I was happy.

The thought of sewing all summer was too much for me. I had heard of a new shearing plant being started on the La Garita and wrote to the man who I considered had the most pull, and asked him to let me feed the men. This was daring, as I was broke and would have to buy all my provisions on credit.

I got the job, contracting to feed the men for fifty cents a meal. This was considered a high price, but, as all my groceries had to be freighted up a steep canyon, I was afraid to try it for less. It was to last but one month — June. Then I began to look for help — there wasn't any. Finally, by coaxing and offering two dollars per day — big wages then — two young girls promised to go. One was an educated, well-bred, very pretty Mexican; the other a white girl — a girl, who in spite of having the cards stacked against her in the way of poverty, lack of home and education, was still making good and who proved a pillar of strength to me. I made out my grocery list — not without misgivings, however, as it was the biggest job I had ever handled. Feeding seventy-five or more men, many of them shearers, who were considered very tough, who traveled, at shearing time, through Montana, Wyoming, Utah, and Colorado. The manager told me to keep a pick handle and hot water in readiness in case they ever went on the rampage as they sometimes did when things did not suit them. They had, so he said, recently started in by throwing ketchup bottles, then beat up the cook, and ended by wrecking both the dining-room and the kitchen. I, too, had seen cooks that would have been better for a few well-thrown ketchup bottles, so I did not worry.

I stopped in Center and had very little trouble getting my groceries on credit; nothing like having influential friends willing to vouch for you. It was a hard grocery order to fill, because it was during the war, and I was rationed on sugar, meat, and flour. We went on to camp. Some of the road was so steep that the boy I was with had to back his Chile line (our name for a small Ford truck) up the hill.

I found a new building made of rough boards nailed on the studding. There was a dining-room, large enough to seat one hundred men;

also a kitchen, a pantry, and two small bedrooms. I had a small cot which was, as far as
comfort was concerned, a delusion and a
snare. The girls had a built-in bunk; on this
they had pine boughs for a mattress. The
kitchen had water piped in from a spring farther up the hill; and to turn it on, I had to use
all my strength besides a pair of pliers; and to
turn it off was almost an impossibility and a
daring deed. Every time we drew water we
scrubbed the floor.

Many of the men were already in camp when
we arrived, and they helped us get settled.
After supper was over, the girls and a group of
men went for a walk and I unpacked as much
as I could. The Company furnished all the
dishes and the cooking utensils, which were
still in their barrels and crates.

Then dark came — but no girls. I had
heard them singing at first; but now it was still
and dark. The men had all gone to the bunk-
house. I was alone in this empty-sounding
building save for the rattle and scurry of mice
and mountain rats. I was very tired and wanted
to turn in; instead I went outside, straining to
hear some sound of the girls. It was very
dark, but I knew they could not be walking
now. At first I was peeved, knowing that with

all this work ahead of us, we should be resting.

Then, as it grew later, I feared they had gone too far before dark and that in this forest of high pine trees had lost their sense of direction. I walked up the mountain-side intending to call; by then I had another worry — those men were all strangers to us, and while personally I had always found men could be trusted, still I knew there were men who could not be. And I was afraid to call, not wanting the other men in the bunk-house to know. There was one there whom I had known for many years, and I walked around and around the bunk-house considering calling him out and getting him to go with me to help hunt. But one of these girls was a Mexican — the other had no mother; now, let a story get started, and neither could ever live it down. I walked the floor wringing my hands, going to the door countless times trying to pierce the darkness; then at ten o'clock I heard them coming, laughing and talking, and I was reassured; it was only youth and a spring night.

I met them at the door, and was crying, though I did not know it; and while I had planned many things to say, all that I could manage was, 'Oh, girls, I've been so worried about you.' Then Millie (I had known her only as a girl who worked around) came to me all in the dark, and said: 'Why, Mrs. Ellis, you are crying. There's been plenty of women mad at me for not getting to bed early so's I could work, but you are the first to shed' (Millie was quite sentimental) 'a single tear or to worry over me, and right here I want to tell you that you won't have to give me another thought.' And I never did. She was ever at my side doing the hardest work, lifting for me, carrying for me. All the hard jobs were Millie's jobs; that comes from being strong and willing. She never hung back one moment in the day; there was nothing too dirty nor too hard for her to do, singing as she went, 'Katy,' 'Mighty like a Rose,' 'Tipperary,' and 'Keep the Home Fires Burning.' She was a born nurse and she was interested in all sickness, especially so in babies, reproduction, sex actions, and reactions. She always wore a nurse's uniform and carried a complete kit of first aid supplies. She had books on sex and the love life which she wished to discuss with Lupie and me. We were hopeless. Lupie, who had the usual Mexican dignity and reserve, changed the subject, while I, rather Victorian, always cringed. Moreover, when the mind is juggling the problems of buying, paying for, and preparing food for seventy-five people, there is no time for sex talk.

In the kitchen were two six-hole ranges placed side by side. One oven did not bake on the bottom and was the cause of much irritation and endless work. All the wood had to be carried either through the dining-room or up a flight of seven steep steps.

Some fool designed this building — I know who he is, and if he ever reads this, his dignity will be ruffled, but not anything like it would have been if he could have heard, as I did, all the curses hurled at him by tired men climbing the steep hill from the shearing plant to the boarding-house. I draped white cheesecloth at each window and used white oilcloth on all the tables. Flags were hung from the rafters and feathery pine boughs were grouped along the studding. Flowers were kept on some of the tables — not on those of the shearers; they wanted only quick service, hot, good strengthening food, and plenty of it, and they were not concerned with flowers or females.

This is the way a day went: I got up at four in the morning — bitter cold in those high altitudes — and built fires in both ranges and put on the breakfast food to cook, cut the bacon — often two slabs — or ham, and put on huge pots of coffee; also huge pans of potatoes to fry. By that time Millie was up and watched the breakfast while I started to make and bake barley biscuits — large pans that just fitted the ovens, filled time and time again. Lupie was up setting the tables, arranging the white enameled plates which had been left on the stove shelf to warm, also putting on the condensed milk, some in the can, some diluted; then butter, fruit (stewed), syrup, preserves, cookies, coffee-cake or doughnuts, and small amounts of sugar. For a while I had the girls pass with the sugar-bowl, giving just so much to each man; but the shearers would not stand for a racket of this kind — war or no war. Then we began frying and boiling eggs — dozens and dozens. Then, if we had time before the men came, we snatched a cup of coffee and a biscuit with orange marmalade. Then it was wild work — I dishing up, both girls rushing, almost running with food to the clammering, yammering, and sometimes — from the shearers' table — hammering men.

I made it a rule — I almost had to, in order to get the work done — that after eating, the men were to stack their dishes, and as they passed out, hand them through an opening into the kitchen. The shearers did it sullenly; anyway, as I quickly piled the dishes, I smiled and spoke to each one. Breakfast was soon over and I went directly to cooking, while the girls washed dishes and peeled potatoes and other vegetables. First I mixed my bread — always hot rolls made of all white or rice flour. Then I made pies, twenty of them, with the crust made of white and barley flour mixed; then, if it was a boil, a stew, or a pot roast, I put the meat to cook. All my meat was bought by the quarter and cut by Millie and myself; once in a while I fed them liver, which they scorned — they did not then know of the strength and nourishment in liver. Neither did I. A pot of soup stock was always going. Before dinner we all washed and changed into clean garments. When dinner dishes were done, the girls could rest for a short time. I went to baking cakes for supper, making every one with barley flour and doing all the sweetening and icing with syrup. They were good cakes, too. For supper I always had hot corn bread — pan after pan. If ever I had a minute, I tried to figure my groceries against the number of meals, marked in a little red book, but it was too discouraging, so I turned all the bookkeeping over to Lupie. I was going on with my job, no matter how it came out. More than anything I missed not having time to read. To read is almost as essential to me as to eat. And I feel far more hunger pangs when I am denied mental nourishment than I do at the loss of meals.

We had our troubles; cold, heat, mice, flies and more flies. I remember once I had a man bring me fourteen hens for a Sunday dinner. (It always fell upon Millie to kill them; all of us helped in the picking and cleaning.) This man started with the chickens in gunny sacks and, coming up the hill, the man, his car, and my chickens all got hot. He, out of the kindness of his heart, dipped the chickens and sacks into the creek to cool them off. When he arrived in camp, he dumped on the ground fourteen chickens, dead, scalded, and picked. No, I did not use them!

The shearers were very exclusive, having a table of their own and pitching their tents a long way from the other men's sleeping quarters. I found them a well-behaved, silent sort — never talking or laughing at the table; only concentrating on eating and doing it as though it were a duty. They were under a terrific strain, working at a high rate of speed — some of them making, so I understood, thirty dollars per day. If I remember correctly, they got seventeen cents for each sheep sheared.

Once they sent the manager to me, telling me they had to have more strengthening food. They wanted steaks twice each day. I felt dreadful, as this was the first time I had heard other than praise for my cooking. It was an impossibility to get more meat. I was then, by coaxing and wheedling, getting more than my war-time allowance. So I decided to feed them all the eggs they could eat and, oh! the cases of eggs that came up that canyon.

Their talk was of sheep, wool, and war. Several of the men were called and left for the training camps. A girl came from town selling war savings stamps. I was daring enough to take fifty dollars' worth, not knowing whether I'd clear that much on the job or not.

Lupie, pretty and charming, was having the time of her life. All the boys, several from the University of Wyoming and from the Colorado Agricultural College, paid her marked attention. One wanted to marry her. There was, too, in the offing, a Mexican sweetheart with a red roadster. Millie, looking out for me, never would let Lupie go beyond calling distance. One evening, during supper, Lupie was talking to an admirer just beyond the door. Both Millie and I were rushing. Millie stopped long enough to hiss to Lupie, 'Better cut it out; do you think Mrs. Ellis is paying you to entertain?'

Lupie almost ran in, and in her quick blaze of anger grabbed a stove-hook and pounded the stove till she broke the hook, then she lifted a large dishpan of water and slammed it on the floor. I stood and looked on, saying nothing; I, too, had had these wild impulses, but never was brave enough to indulge them; besides it wasn't my stove-hook; the floor got a scrubbing, and everybody was relieved.

For this one month all our lives were sheep-filled. Day and night we talked, smelled, thought, listened to, and saw sheep; endless bleating sheep, coming like waves over the bare hill below camp. Lucky were the first bands, because there was no grass for those following. The herders came rattling rocks in tin cans, others waving gunny sacks, were aided by dogs, which many times showed more intelligence than the sheep or the herders, in trying to get them corralled.

Only once or twice did I find time to visit

[113]

the plant, so I am not sure of my knowledge. This, as I remember, was the process of shearing: The sheep, after being run in, are separated from the young lambs; then those to be sheared the next day are run, with much noise and swearing in Mexican, into the sweating-room. This is supposed to make shearing easier. The next morning they are driven — a goat to lead them — up a chute into a large room. Off this room are many chutes, each of which is just wide enough for a single sheep. At the top of each chute is a door opening outward into the shearing-room. The herders keep the chutes full of sheep. There is a constant beat of reverberating bleats from the young lambs, answered by the anxious, frightened ewes. The shearing-room is very large with smooth hardwood floors. Along them, hanging down on pliable cords, are the clippers. The power is turned on — the shearers stand almost stripped to the waist. At the right of each one are two little doors, one opening in, the other out. There is so much noise, you fairly rock with it. Then with a sweep of his arm every shearer reaches for a sheep that is either pushed or pulled through the doors that open inward. With almost one motion the animal is secured limply between his

knees and legs, and the clippers are running
over it. In just a moment, it seems, the bare,
bony, and often bloody sheep is thrown and
pushed through the door that opens outward,
unless it is cut too badly. In this case the
wound is sewed up with common sewing thread.
To each shearer there was allotted a boy to
pick up and carry away the fleece which has
come off the sheep in almost a single mat.
It is then carried to the wool classer's table,
where it is judged and graded; then put into
its proper bin. It then goes, I think, to the
sacking and weighing machine; then is sten-
ciled with the weight, the grade, the owner's
name, also the sheep brand. It is after this
loaded for the haul to the railroad. This
particular wool, I believe, the Government
took and held in warehouses indefinitely, and
if they ever paid for it at all, it was a small
amount. This almost broke our county sheepmen.

All day that went on. The shearers very
seldom straightened up; endless lines of sheep
were pulled through doors, then clipped, and
thrust back through other doors. When the
clipped sheep came from the shearing-room,
they were run through other chutes, while
men with brushes and buckets of paint marked

them with their sign or brand on their hides.

Then, and only then, are they turned to their starving lambs — many ewes will not own their lambs; then this band or bunch — none of them have been fed during this procedure — are started up the gulch toward the summer range on the high peaks. One night, after a cold rain, the weakened, newly sheared sheep died by the hundreds. In the morning the ground was covered with mounds which looked like heaps of dirty snow. Another night something frightened them in the sweating-pen (a sheep has no sense), and they piled upon each other and many were smothered.

The bands belonged to different owners and the different owners and their herders came and went with their sheep.

Now I don't know whether or not every unmarried woman — whether maid or widow — is always waiting, looking for, and expecting her King or Prince Charming. I do know that one was. Always, when she heard of a new man coming into the community, she thought, 'this might be the one'; always when he proved to be likable, she was disappointed to hear him speak of his wife.

This one I knew had enough sense to realize the Prince Charming she was looking for would not pick his wife from the kitchen. Anyway, I had made inquiries about the different sheep-owners. One seemed very eligible — a gentleman, educated, well-to-do, and well liked. I had never seen him, but decided when his sheep were run through to do my best in the way of cooking. I had even saved a good-looking dress to wear on this occasion. Lupie kept track of and checked the meals. The owners and herders paid when leaving. The shearers and all other help were to pay at the end of the job. One morning Lupie said: 'There's a man been eating here. I did not get his name, and I see he's getting ready to leave with his band of sheep, and he's never mentioned pay.' Now Millie had her say, 'You're a great bookkeeper, I'll say. Now I bet, if I was doing it, no guy would put it over on me.' Lupie said, 'Why don't you do it, then? You have my full permission.' 'Well, you can't bluff me,' Millie replied. 'I just will'; and she went down the hill. I was frying doughnuts, my head tied up in a cloth which hid my hair, my greatest asset. I was losing this because of bending over hot stoves so many hours each day. I was warm and red-faced;

then from a man standing in the door (he had the brownest eyes and nicest voice), 'I did not intend to leave before paying — perhaps, though, it's just as well you reminded me.' And he smiled and handed me a check. After he was gone, I looked at it and found the name of the man whom I had been so anxious to please.

Oh, well, ''twas ever thus.' I wonder if others are like this? I can look back now, a few years or months or days even, and see when I was thoughtless, silly, and inadequate, and can smile at myself.

The last week on the job I thought, 'I just can't get up this morning and go through with it.' I did, though. It was on the Fourth of July that we finished. I left with over a thousand dollars in checks and cash. On the road at noon we stopped in La Garita; and we went into the store and bought canned peaches, sardines, and crackers. And it was the best meal I had eaten in a month. When my debts were paid, I had a few hundred dollars left. I felt proud and had more confidence in myself. At once I had my teeth attended to — teeth I had let go for many years when I lived in mining camps far from a dentist. I had doctored some of them myself, often burning out the aching nerves with carbolic acid.

About ten days before we finished, a man injured his hand dreadfully. At once Millie had out her kit and washed, dressed, and bandaged it for him in a workmanlike manner. Afterward, I said to a professor who taught in the University of Wyoming and who was present, 'It's too bad Millie can't have training; she is a born nurse.' He asked why she could not. I told him that ever since she was a little girl, she had been compelled to work, only being able to go to school between jobs; consequently, she did not have the number of high-school credits required for entrance. That day he said no more. Later he came to me and asked if I thought, given the chance, Millie would go into training and make good. I assured him that she would. Then he made arrangements for her to go to the University of Wyoming. She was bubbling with delight, singing as she worked, 'I'm so happy, so very, very, happy, so happy —— ' I don't know whether this was a real song or only a Millie song.

Lupie, leaving several disappointed white boys, rode off with her Mexican sweetheart in the red roadster and Millie went with me.

Then we prepared her clothes and planned. She went to Denver and was to go on to Wyoming in the fall. I did not hear from her, and I feared our plans were too hard to carry out. It was over a year after when I did hear that she had, in her good-hearted way, given her money to a needy relative; then had worked and saved another year in order to go. This she did, graduating in due time, and taking her place in the world. I wonder where she is today? Wherever it is, she is serving humanity cheerfully and efficiently, unless — she was so good-hearted — the love life, about which she had wished to talk, has not been too much for her.

CHAPTER VIII

Even the highest office in the land is not 'conferred.' It is
bargained for, bought, traded, stolen, sold. It is not the will
of the people. It is big business backed by unlimited money,
and by people of power with political axes to grind.

A. E.

AFTER the shearing-plant job was over, I had
some dentistry done, and before it was finished,
I had another job, cooking for a hay crew.
And the moment the bridge was clamped into
my mouth, I climbed into a car and went to
this ranch. To any one suffering with new
bridges or teeth, I should recommend cooking
for ten or twelve men. You haven't time to
think, 'Do they hurt, or don't they?' or,
'Can I stand it, or can't I?'

The work-filled days passed. One noon for
dessert I was having lemon pie, also mince
pie with hard sauce, and, to gladden the Mexicans' hearts, a few drops of whiskey in it.

The platter of méringue I was whipping for
the lemon pie was in its last stages of white
fluffiness — when — crash! I knew it was an
automobile wreck on the high graded road, and
I ran, never missing a stroke, whipping the
frosting. I saw that a new Ford truck had gone

head-on into a large rock beside the road.
The driver was out looking at the damage.
He came on down the hill, talking in his usual
cheerful, spluttering manner. It was Boss
M——, our town's richest and best-liked man
— a power in politics.

Still whipping the egg whites, I said, 'Well,
Boss, so it's you disturbing the peace?' He
broke in: 'Sister, I've about ruined my Chile
line, can't see how I done it. Can't see how it
happened. The rocks are too near the road,
that's what; rocks are too near the road. No
man could miss 'em; where's your 'phone?'
I showed him and went on with my dinner.
He called a garage to bring repairers, then a
road gang to fix the road.

I was glad for the chance of a visit with Boss
M——, as he was always kind and friendly to
me and could pass out many favors. I thought
he might get me on the election board for the
coming election. I said, 'Now you must stay
for dinner'; then I added, 'I'm glad it was you
who ran into that rock; now maybe there will
be something done about it.' He answered,
'That's right — there will.' Then I went on,
'Tell me all the news; what's doing in politics?'
I went on with my dinner and we talked. He
told me who was nominated for each office. We

talked over each one's chances for election, and why he could or could not be elected — and, during this whole afternoon, neither the political boss nor I, the average voter, said one word about the candidate's fitness for office, only — 'Can he be elected?'

I felt very proud that Boss M—— was telling me all these intimate party details, although in my heart I knew he was only telling just as much as he wanted repeated. He told me it was hard to get any one to run against the County Treasurer, because he was a hard man to beat.

They had, he said, a good man for Assessor; also for County Clerk; but when he told me who was running for Clerk, I said, 'He'll never make it.' Boss M—— could not see why, as the man was well liked, he belonged to a large family, and was popular.

I had overheard Mexicans talking of not getting a square deal from him when he was a bartender, but I did not tell Boss M—— that. I only said, 'He's all right, but — I'll bet he won't win; why I would stand more of a chance of winning than he.' At this Boss M—— looked quickly at me, but said nothing — he was too good a politician to argue with any one.

This was in July, when we finished haying on the lower ranch, we moved the cook outfit, men, horses, and machinery, to a ranch farther up the creek.

One day my men were in for dinner. They had washed, waiting their turn for the tin washpans and towels — then, after slicking their fingers through their wet hair, they were soon sitting around the long table on chairs, boxes, and on a bench at the back of the table. They, as they always did, had passed the cream from hand to hand, each one covering his saucer of pie full to the brim.

Everything was on the table except the meat. I was carving huge thin slices of rare roast beef. I had filled one large platter, covering it with brown gravy, and was starting to carve another platterful, when the telephone rang. I answered it, thinking it was for Clyde, the manager.

It was hard to hear. I held one hand over my ear to shut out the noise at the table.

Then I heard faintly — it was a banker from Center: 'Mrs. Ellis, we are coming up to see you later in the day; I just called to tell you that you are nominated for County Treasurer.' I broke in, 'Just now I'm too busy to joke, call me later.' 'But,' he said, 'I am not

joking. We are very anxious that you accept.'
My men were rattling dishes, clamoring for
meat, and I just had to wait on them. Then,
again, the insistent, persuasive voice, 'Please
say you will accept.' 'All right,' I said. I
knew I must get to those hungry men. 'Call
me in an hour or two.' I hung up the receiver,
and, with my heart beating high, fairly flew,
carving meat, refilling coffee-cups and bread
plates, thinking, 'It's crazy... As soon as the
men are in the fields, I'll call and fix it all
straight ... the very idea; I must have heard
wrong; things like this don't happen to me.'
Yet, inside, I was warm with pleasure. Finally
the men were finished and were rubbing their
hands in a satisfied fullness. Most of them, to
please me, gathered their empty dishes and,
as they passed out, piled them on another
table.

I never ate till they were gone; then I could
do it in peace and quietness. That day, I
was too nervous to eat; planning, when they
called me, just what to say; how to refuse.
Before I was fairly started on my dishes, the
telephone rang; it was my son. 'Why, Mamma,
what's this I hear about you? You're not going
into politics, I hope?' I was ruffled and said,
'Why not?' Why, Mamma, no woman's

ever been elected in this county, and Will Sloan is such a good man.' I knew all this too well; but I said, 'I'd like to have you know I'm a good woman, and furthermore, I'm running!' I hung up and returned to the unwashed dishes. I was a little worried by then. Again the telephone was ringing, my daughter this time. 'Mamma Annie, we understand you have accepted the nomination for treasurer; do you consider this wise?' Rather sharply I said, 'Certainly I do; this is just the right time.' (I should have said psychological, only at this time I did not know there was such a word.) Neita went on: 'You will have to make the campaign, which will be expensive.' I broke in, 'I have considered all that' (what a liar!), 'but I have the money from my shearing-plant job and I believe I can make it; I am going to run, so there!' Then, much more worried, I returned to the fast-cooling dishwater, wishing they would let me alone. If I got the dishes done, the bread and the cakes baked, and had supper on the table at six, there was no time for telephone conversation.

For the third time the telephone rang. I went, wiping my hands on my apron, and almost grabbed the receiver from the hook. 'Hello — Hello' comes the soft voice of my

sister-in-law. 'Annie, how are you this lovely
day? It's too beautiful to be indoors, isn't it?'
I admitted it, and waited. 'Why, Annie, we
have heard the most interesting news of you.'
I said, 'Yeh?' and waited. 'We did not know
you were considering politics and we wonder if
you have weighed it well. No woman has ever
been elected, and Mr. Sloan is such a nice man
with a nice family, and you know he is a college
graduate — from the State University, you
know — while you —— ' This hurt; besides, I
had supper to get. I answered, 'They all want
me to run. I am a nice woman with a nice
family, and with them all working for me I believe I have a chance. You have a lot of influence' (she did too) — 'get busy.'

I turned from the telephone and sat down
weakly; my tired hands dropped into my lap.
My first thought was, 'All this wasted time; I
never can get my bread and cakes baked before supper.' I reached to the door-facing and
pulled myself up and, glancing at my bread,
discovered it was running over the sides of the
pans. This brought me out of it in a hurry and
my movements raced, building the fire, getting the oven ready — working against time.

I had a gone feeling, and my thoughts were
racing too: 'Now there may be a chance; the

few hundred dollars I have aren't much —
maybe now if I could put this over, I could
keep Earl in school. It will be fun electioneering — I could play I was having a vacation.
I believe I will!' By the time the bread was
out and the cakes in, I had planned my clothes
and was busy on my speech of acceptance; and
it was supper-time before I realized that I had
not eaten since breakfast. Then I thought,
'Why did I commit myself? How foolish! But
now, I must go on. Could I do it, should I try
it, would I ever learn to control my tongue?
What a fool! and to think I had, all the days of
my life, to live with this fool!'

At night I told the men; they laughed, and
even the Mexicans smiled. Then they encouraged me.

Later in the evening a committee called on
me. I said to one of them, a banker, 'But,
Simpson, you know I don't know enough to be
Treasurer.' He said (which was not the right
answer at all): 'You don't have to know anything. Why, once there was a man elected, and
he was such a drunk that they never even let
him have the key to the office; you just get a
good deputy and you can manage. I feel sure
we can elect you.'

At the time I thought that they had my

interests at heart — that it was me they wanted to help, and that I would be of service to the county. Gosh! Candidates, from City Marshal to President, are first chosen on their chance of being elected!

I went right on cooking for the hay hands until a month before election. One day, through the window, I saw the men coming; they were leading and dragging a Mexican covered with blood. I went quietly on about my work, thinking it might be a fight, in which, since I was in politics, I did not care to take a hand. They went on into the bunk-house. Soon Mr. Clyde, my rich, educated, rather spoiled employer, with his handsome face very pale, was standing in the doorway rolling his sleeves up.

'Annie, there's been an accident; the bar on the mowing machine sprang back and I think knocked out an eye for Francisco. Get me some cloths, will you, please, while I get the water.' Without a word I tore up a white petticoat (we still wore them then), handed it to him, and went on about my business. In a moment Clyde was back in the doorway holding to the facing for support. 'Annie, I can't do it — it sickens me — I wonder if you can.'

I took the cloth and basin and went to the bunk-house to find Francisco sitting up on the

edge of a bunk, his head split wide open, an
eye out upon his cheek, and blood just streaming to the floor. All the other Mexicans were
squatting mutely around the walls. I gave
Francisco, who was not even grunting, one
look; then went to the door and called, 'Clyde,
I know you have a bottle of whiskey in your
room. Francisco needs it. Bring a glassful.'
He did, after fortifying himself. I handed it to
Francisco, who could not speak English. He
drank it at almost a gulp, washing it down
with his own blood which ran and dripped into
the glass. The others licked their lips, and, as
near as a Mexican can, looked envious.

Then I washed and tied him up the best I
could, and helped him till the doctor came.
Although such a thing was never mentioned or
even thought of, there is no telling how many
votes this made for me. Weeks before election,
Francisco, who, after all, did not lose his eye,
sent his young daughter to me, telling me that
she was to go with me to the Mexican homes
and do my talking.

Now at this time I was ignorant of county
affairs — the average woman is. Taxes, to me,
were a nightmare, something that you saved
for, in order to pay if you could; nothing to
worry over if you couldn't. I didn't know who,

why, or how they arrived at the amount on my tax card. When the Assessor made his rounds, we had a pleasant visit; I, with pride, insisting my furniture and house were worth more than he thought. When I did not like a school teacher, I complained of paying my taxes toward her support, although I had no idea how my twenty dollars were apportioned. I now know many teachers, too, who do not know this, and who blame the school board for not raising their wages.

One day Clyde stopped me. I suppose he wanted to know what my reactions, if any, were. (This writing is the first time I have ever confessed to any thoughts beyond the day's work.) I was always sensitive, not sure of myself, so, outwardly, often played the fool. However, in politics it pays to have people think you know less than you do. Clyde said to me: 'Well, Annie, what's the first thing you are going to do if you're elected?' Neither of us expected I would be, but it was pleasant to plan.

I answered: 'Just this: I've never had a good bed. I'm going to have a real bed. I've never had a boughten dress; I'm going to Denver and buy a real one. And I've never been in a beauty parlor nor had my hands manicured.

I'm going into one and tell them to shoot the works.' He said — he thought he was a sophisticated iconoclast — 'And have you no thought of purity in politics? Nor what a woman's influence might mean?'

Yes. In my heart I had thought of just that, and I wanted and expected to help; but I wasn't going to tell this scoffer so. I just smiled.

He went on: 'Of course your faith is in Elmer, the all-highest, who — he thinks — rules the party. A moral man.' This I knew was sarcasm, as the very least Clyde ever said of Elmer was to apply to him such adjectives as 'supercilious,' 'pusillanimous,' attached to a name not meant for polite ears. At the time I resented this; later, however, when I was better acquainted with Elmer, I found it was a mild term for him.

Naturally there was much talk. My brother-in-law, the boss on the telephone job, said about the most pertinent thing: 'She has about as much chance as a snowball in hell. If she did have it, what in the name of God would she do with it?'

One night, after supper, Clyde took me to town, and I attended my first meeting and put up the money for my campaign fund. This was a love feast, each candidate telling the other, 'How glad I am you are on the ticket because you will give it strength. You have so many friends, you boost for me among them, and I'll pull for you among mine. I sure do have influence.' And so on. There were no real arrangements made, as I supposed there would be. Those, I was later to learn, were made in meetings attended by the wise and politically elect. I never did get in on one. Women I imagine, in county, state, or national politics very seldom — if ever — see the inside workings of the political machine. They are too apt at throwing monkey-wrenches.

I held my job till the first of October, then I started to electioneer. I am a natural-born politician, because I like and am interested in all people and neither look up to nor down upon any one.

For instance, some time ago on the train I made the acquaintance of a William J. Long of Stamford, Connecticut, who is a writer of textbooks on literature. In speaking to him of some one writing (not me), I said, 'The life so short — the art so long to learn.' He told me Chaucer wrote it. I did not know, my knowledge is so patchy. Then he quoted from many writers. It was a lovely visit. Not an hour afterwards, the gray-haired Negro porter and I were having just as wonderful a visit over his and his wife's efforts to obtain a home.

I am always good-natured and neither praise nor blame has any effect on me, except that of amusement. This is an asset in politics, where it doesn't pay to be thin-skinned.

One of my mottoes is, 'Never be sniffy to any one — you never know when you might want that vote.'

CHAPTER IX

Politics not only makes bedfellows of strangers, but strangers
of bedfellows.

My Sister Jose

I HAD a blue suit just right for a campaign. It
was cheap and looked it. It was also trim and
neat — nothing to excite pity or envy. This I
wore with plain white shirt waists. Once when
I was out longer than I expected and my collar and cuffs were soiled, I turned the waist
wrong side out, and the people at the dance
wondered why I wore my coat all evening.

Saguache County is very large. I went to
every town, mining camp, ranch, and sheep
camp; and talked to business men, housewives,
potato-diggers, and threshing-machine gangs.
I called at every place; upon Democrats as well
as Republicans. If I knew they were not going
to vote for me, the more I enjoyed the call.

There was nothing I could say against my
opponent — he was very efficient and honest;
except that he had a job and I wanted it.

Before I started, I had a talk with myself (I
often do). Sometimes, after I've gone to bed,
I scold myself, thinking — 'You old fool, just

why did you say that? Will you never control your tongue?' In this election campaign, I thought, 'No matter what comes up, or how it turns out, you are to take it cheerfully and bravely.' So I did not go at it hammer and tongs, nor, as some do, almost making it a matter of life or death.

I had never had a vacation in my life, so I decided to call this one, and I enjoyed every minute of it. Autumn in Colorado is a most wondrous time.

I never asked for a vote nor asked people how they were going to vote. I made it a practice to visit awhile, saying, 'Of course you know why I am here — I just thought I'd come and let you see what I look like, and tell you I will appreciate anything you can do for me.' They, in turn, never promised a vote; only, 'Well, if I can't do you any good, I won't do you any harm'; or, 'I'll do what I can, but you don't stand a ghost of a show.'

I hesitated about talking to men at work on their jobs. Men at their work don't like it any too well to be stopped by a candidate electioneering, especially if the candidate is a woman; they instinctively feel that she is out of her place, and, maybe she is. Women are queer. I know one who was frantic for woman's suffrage. She was in the big Equal Rights Parade in New York, led, I think, by Margaret Illington on a large white horse. There were so many marching women that it took six hours for it to pass. At a recent election this woman failed to vote and had even forgotten it was election day. Moreover, to add to men's disgust, I carried no cigars, and there is no point in a politician visiting without cigars.

There were many dances which were attended by the candidates on both sides. For those dances I always stopped campaigning long enough to fry huge quantities of doughnuts — my share of the midnight supper. At fairs or public sales, all the candidates were out in full force.

Bonanza, my old home town, has always taken its politics seriously and Democratically. When I called the Republican committeeman to make arrangements, he told me there was no use to come to town, as there weren't even enough Republicans there to get the hall ready. I insisted upon going, and for the Republican dance, meeting, and supper, the Democrats had to make all of the arrangements.

Talk about a prophet (or a politician) in his own country! When I started in the political game, all those Bonanza people thought it a joke. You see they had known me so long and so well. Then, too, they resented, just as I probably should have done had I been one of them, my taking a few steps forward.

Also, they thought, 'She will have the big-head if she's ever elected.' (I might have thought the same of them.)

Of course, I had my steadfast friends who stood by me, but even they thought I was being used as a tool. I didn't care. I was willing to be elected as a tool, because tools, like worms, sometimes turn.

I will say right here that I never did carry Bonanza.

Sometime I should like to write about Bonanza's elections. Just now I call to mind that once, years ago, when I was keeping boarders in Bonanza, Joy, my little girl, knew I was getting ready for the candidates. When they came, and Joy understood those were the long-expected candidates, she cried and said, 'Why, they are only men!'

It seems she thought we had said 'candy dates,' and thought they were some kind of a confection. In those days candidates came in buggies and had plenty of whiskey with them.

They would take up headquarters at one of the saloons and give the saloon a certain amount of money to treat the men.

I little thought then that some day I, too, would be a candidate — or that, when I was one, the hardest thing to believe would be that sometime I should write of it. 'Life is so full of a number of things ——'

Once, long before my campaign, all the candidates of both parties were snowed in at Bonanza for three days, and such times! One day the Republicans were in the lead; then next, the Democrats held the floor. All the time there was a big poker game in full blast. Very likely the newcomers thought they were putting it over on the miners.

On this trip the politicians had left their whiskey jugs in a cabin near us, and the candidate for County Judge stayed to watch it. When the others returned to the base of supply, they found him on the floor dead drunk and curled around the jugs. He had to be worked with all night to bring him out of it.

Somehow, in the old days, politicians knew their cards; still, I'll bet when they left town most of the cash was in the pockets of Long John, Slippery Joe, or Picnic Jim, who knew theirs better.

So, as some one has said, 'That cheerful, clever, kindly creature, the candidate, is with us once more.' It would be well, I think, if each and every one of us were running for office continuously, we are so friendly, so concerned about every one's welfare; going out of our road to speak and be pleasant to people; doing many kindnesses that otherwise we should leave undone. We do not realize it, but I suppose in a way we are running for office, only the day of vote-counting is far distant — maybe.

Naturally in my campaign I made many mistakes. Recently I read where a man gave ten rules for making a fool of one's self. To these I could add more that I have used with great success.

For instance, when I visited Bonanza, going up with the candidate for Assessor in his open Ford truck, it was cold and I wrapped myself to the eyes in a thick quilt. After our house-to-house calls in Bonanza, we next visited the Rawley mine, which was two and a half miles from town.

On one mile of this road I had traveled barefoot thousands of times in summer and in winter, going from the little school in Bonanza to Exchequer, where we lived.

This time it was on one of those wonderful fall days that I have seen in no place except Colorado; the air warm, mellow, and mild; the green, golden, yellow, orange, and crimson quaking asp crowding the road to greet me. Squirrel Creek, which I could seldom see for the sturdy alders and overhanging willows, gurgled and sang to me; rosebushes beside the road waved red berries at me. I was happy.

I rode up with the men, but I wanted to walk back alone — I wanted to bathe my mind in memories. Every step was history — my family history. We had picked berries here; hunted watercress there; a bed of primroses grew in that place; and here was a spot under a pine tree where I had been given — and gave — my first kiss. Then — I was brought back over thirty years by some one shouting to me. I looked up the hill to see men grading a road just back of where our old house used to stand.

They yelled, and waved their arms at me. I waved and called back, thinking, 'How nice of them! They know who I am and what I am running for; perhaps some one among them remembers me from a little barefoot girl when I used to hunt cows over every one of these hills; and now they are friendly and are shouting to let me know that I will get every one of their votes.' They shouted and waved their arms harder than ever. Again I waved. Then they began to run, calling as they ran. I ran, too, and jumped for the willows, throwing myself underneath their protecting branches as the world shook with a terrific blast; and rocks, dirt, and huge boulders rained down, around and over me. When the smoke had cleared away, I crawled out, dusted myself off, and without one backward glance went down the road and away from there, a sadder, and a wiser, politician. I knew that I was being roundly damned by those miners, whose lives as well as my own I had so lately endangered.

I tried to make a house-to-house canvass; this is harder than peddling, because you meet with the same rebuffs and coldness, and you never know till the votes are counted whether you have sold yourself or not.

Very often you would be surprised if you knew who did vote for you and more than surprised if you knew who did not. I used to lie awake nights — after traveling all day — and take the towns, street by street, house by house, and weigh each prospective voter one by one.

Every person is a factor in politics. True, he

has but one vote, but he can influence many more, unless, as Mark Twain said of the mummy, he's 'a dead one not able to vote.'

Among the foolish things I did — and they were many — this stands out in my mind. We were in Center and had been standing around in the stores meeting and talking to the people as they came in to trade. I could see that I was not getting very far with this, because people on business bent are not in the right frame of mind to be approached politically.

I saw several cars passing all filled with women; as one drew to the curb, I asked the woman who was driving where they were going; she told me several miles out to a farm where the Ladies' Aid were giving a dinner. I asked her if I might go and climbed into her already crowded car.

It was the usual Ladies' Aid; tired, pleasant-faced women bringing in and unwrapping their food, either boastfully or bashfully, apologetically or approvingly. After dinner they had a business meeting; the business, as it ever seems to be, was how to raise funds for various purposes. I wanted my chance and called aside the one whom I considered the best talker, and I told her that in electioneering I never treated, I never bought cigars, and so on, but that I had enjoyed their meeting and would like to help, and if they could use five dollars I'd gladly give it. She thought they could, and got up excitedly and told the crowd who I was and what I was running for. I was warm inside — this was putting it over. Then, in a last burst of enthusiasm, she suggested that they give me a standing vote of thanks — and I — I, in my pleased nervousness, before all those whom I wanted to impress, was the first to stand on my feet. And then, to add to my chagrin, and the irony of it, I found each and every one of them voted in another county.

Another time, I, with other candidates, was talking to some men who were working on a section gang; I was showing off a little, I expect, displaying the stand-in I had with the Mexicans. I met Abato; he and I were particular friends, both of us having suffered from hay fever while we were once working on the same job, he in the fields, I as cook. At that time he was in love with a young girl whose mother, Cita, if ever a woman did, had 'it.' Cita was charming. There's no one I'd rather talk to or have smile at me than Cita. Underbred Latins have a natural grace of manner that underbred Nordics lack. She had had several husbands, interspersed with lovers. She was more than twice as old as Abato, but in spite of this she cut out her daughter and married him. I knew all this very well; but this day, Abato being so friendly, telling me he would swing a good many votes my way, all must have gone to my head. Then he said, 'Come on up to the house and meet my wife.' And I, never thinking, just talking as I am prone to do, said, 'How nice! Why, Abato, you don't mean to say you have a wife old enough to vote?' This was too much even for a Mexican's calm, and he replied, 'God, yes! It's Cita.'

One night I stayed at a third-grade boarding-house, which was filled with men, potato-diggers, sheepmen, railroad hands — more votes here than in a better-class place. It was full-up. Finally I got a cot in the hall of an attic where only men slept. I went to bed in the dark before any of them came in. In this whole world filled with fears I have but two, and neither of these fears is of men — drunk or sober. All night long it seemed that men tramped by my bed; young men and old men, Mexicans, and white men, most of them quietly, all without even glancing at me. Before daylight I sat up on the cot and dressed, combed my hair the best I could without a mirror. I never carried a vanity case; while I'm not superstitious, still, I don't want to break any mirrors! Then I powdered my face — still in the dark — and blacked my eyebrows with a burned match, and I was ready for a new day.

I was electioneering without much advice from any one. My friends were not very enthusiastic; many of them thought I was on the ticket to fill up space and to be traded.

The central committee, so far as I could see, were not especially interested. Several times I asked some one of them for advice, and he would say: 'Just get out and meet the people — that's about all you can do. Of course, whenever you can, put in a word for the rest of the ticket.'

At first I tried this, but I found I lost ground explaining that it was a perfect ticket. Besides, I've never seen one. In talking to men, I tried to keep away from political issues; you see, like the average woman, I have only a headline knowledge of so many things.

Once I stopped at a ranch house where the County Demonstrator was showing several

women how to make a dress form by pulling a
tight knitted garment over the head, then
wrapping and pasting a million — I think —
yards of paper tape around the live figure.
When it is properly dried, the mummy case is
slit up the front and a perfect reproduction of
the wearer is the result.

Those women were all Democrats. I knew it
before I went, and naturally when I broke in on
their meeting, I was none too welcome. Anyway, I went in, and was much interested in all
they were doing; I never mentioned politics.
Then, when the time was ripe, I pulled up my
dress and showed them my petticoat made of
three pairs of old silk stockings, split, turned
ankle-end up, fagoted together, and trimmed
with tiny hand-made French flowers. I had
their attention, and, if I never made a vote, at
least they felt friendly toward me.

All this time I had no idea of the importance
of the Treasurer's office. It was a good thing,
too, that I didn't. The campaign was almost
over before I knew that the Treasurer handled
a large amount of money. This I learned by a
white-haired rancher coming up to the car
where I was sitting. Looking intently at me, he
said, 'I've always voted her straight, but now
I don't know; I wonder if you're capable of

handling the county money — being a woman, and all.

I laughed and said, 'Better try it and see.' He went on, 'Since I've seen you, I guess I will.' I must have looked more capable than I felt. I was beginning to realize, that the Treasurer's office was one of the most important in the county; also I was beginning to wonder if there might not be a 'nigger in the woodpile.'

As election time drew near, I saw that my chances for winning were slim. This I told some of the leaders, and asked them if it would not be well to choose some one for my deputy in case I was elected, and let them get busy and throw all the votes possible our way. Every time I mentioned this, I was put off and told, 'Leave all that to us; we have been in politics a long time and know the game from start to finish.' So I went on with a face drawing, from a forced smile; my lips prim, from saying, 'appreciate.' My family and my friends were all working for me; also a husband and wife I had worked for in a former election gave up their business and took to the field. And my Mexican friends were rallying around me. A few enemies of my opponent were also in the fight — people will work harder to defeat an enemy than they will to elect a friend.

I could see, though, that this was not enough to elect me, and I was worried. I decided to play politics on my own hook. Without advice from any one, I decided to make a move. I ran over in my mind the people who I thought would make good deputies from the standpoint of ability, energy, good sense, and — yes, votes. I decided upon a young widow who was working in a store to support herself and her baby.

It was late in the evening when I went to see her. She was sweeping her porch, and when I called her, she leaned on one side of the gate and I on the other. I said, 'Jean, if I'm elected here, would you like to be my deputy?' She laughed nervously, partly in surprise, partly because she thought it absurd of me ever considering being elected. I am naturally flippant, but as I talked on, she saw that this time I was in earnest. I told her that she would make more than she was then getting; and that it would not be such hard work. So we stood, she switching up little flicks of dust with the broom. Then she said to me — there is no telling what she said to herself — 'All right.'

I told her every vote was going to count and
to call her brothers — both strong Democrats
— and tell them she was to be deputy and they
must act accordingly. We decided to keep this
secret. The following day, the day before election, how she did work on every person who
went into the store! The brothers were working for me in different parts of the county, and
when a Democrat comes out flat-footed for a
Republican, it counts!

At a meeting held just before election, where
ways and means were discussed — nothing
helpful as far as I could see — each one, except
me, sure of election, was telling of promised
landslides, of leading the ticket and so on.
The chairman had prepared letters to send to
each precinct too late for the Democrats to
have a comeback. So far as the Republican
candidates were concerned, these letters were
complimentary — unduly so; while the Democrats were roasted. I admitted not knowing
much of the game, but I did object to those
letters; thinking it was beside the question
whether a man had paid his debts promptly,
or had looked on the wine when it was red, or
had not wanted to go to war. None of our
well-to-do young men had gone to war, and I
said so. Another member of the committee

was of my opinion, and they promised us — or I thought they did — not to send those letters.

But on the evening before election, a staunch Democrat who had been on one of our telephone jobs came to my door — just faunching and spluttering. 'I didn't think it of you — that you'd send out a dirty letter like that.' I asked, although I knew, 'What letter?' He stammered, getting redder and madder: 'You never did stand much show, and writing a thing like that sure's put the skids under you. I thought I wouldn't take a hand either way, but, now I will, and I can sure lose you a few votes.'

He went home grumbling, and I went into the house and baked a pan of corn bread — his weakness. After dark I went to his cabin with it. At first he wasn't going to let me in, but as I talked and explained as much as I felt I could without getting the party in wrong, he cooled down. I stayed quite a while, not mentioning votes, just visiting over our old jobs. The next morning early, before the polls had opened, here he came, carrying in his hand a jar of beets he had put up. I knew they were a peace offering, but I never did know how he voted.

There is one precinct in our county of mostly

Mexican voters, a precinct which has decided many elections. Here I've heard that money talks. I don't know — as none of mine did. I've heard of a shrewd politician rolling a ten-dollar bill around the outside of one dollar bills till the roll was large and convincing; then putting several of these rolls into different pockets, so that they showed. This discouraged the other side so that they gave up early in the game. In this precinct, candidates and workers stay all night before election, and all of election day. Here it was that the husband and wife, who were working for me, got in their best licks.

Election morning, I was up and out early — firing workers with my own enthusiasm. I was always walking, sometimes almost running, as I step quickly. I never got into a car. Let the others ride — I found more votes on foot.

Before the polls opened, I was given a telegram that almost ruined me before I read it. You see, telegrams in our family meant something serious and were only sent in case of sickness or death. I trembled so I could hardly open it; then I was relieved and happy to find it was from the Armstrongs, wishing me luck on election day.

I'm sure that in larger towns they do not have the fun and excitement that we do where there is but one voting place. Cars dash up and down, hauling voters to the polls and home again; many people being 'taken for a ride' who must, between elections, go on shanks' mares. Groups of men are on every corner; and hurrying, polite politicians are everywhere.

I dashed down one street, spoke pleasantly to every one in speaking distance; and hurried on, leading them to think that I was intent on important business. Then I slipped down an alley and dashed down another street; talking to workers and candidates, asking, 'How is it going?' Often I passed the jolly, silk-shirted, warm-overcoated, cigar-smoking candidate for Clerk; also I went by his opponent, in his thin, old, mended, unpressed suit, standing overcoatless, smiling his wistful (and clever) smile — raking in the votes.

If election day is a cold day, it is considered lucky for Democrats, because — they say — they are not so thin-skinned as Republicans. This day was cool, and by noon we heard we were not doing so well. This news can leak out, I don't know how. I have heard of people who were doing the counting (shut up in a tight room), holding up, in front of a window, a certain number of fingers.

Some people, on hearing they are losing, lie down on the job. I never do. I worked at this election up to the time the polls closed; then went quietly home with a feeling of relief, knowing that next morning I should not have to take to the road.

After supper, several of us were to meet at the home of the silk-shirted candidate for Clerk. He was the one whom I had told Boss M—— stood no show of election; but, as the campaign went on, he himself was so sure, his friends so confident, that I began to doubt my judgment. Then the returns began to come in. These, after all, are what count. They were all running better than I. More returns. I was picking up a little. Some had gained enough so that they had passed the losing point.

Then it looked as though I had a chance. I was really getting excited, as deep in my heart I had never expected to win.

Then we knew that the one who was so dead sure had lost. He was walking the floor, swearing — talking of being traded and double-crossed. (I've never known a man to be beaten fairly, nor one to be elected, unfairly.) The beaten clerk's wife went to bed with hysterics.

So, he who had lost, and they who had won, and I who was doubtful, went home tired, disillusioned, and discouraged — and so to bed.

The next morning, before I was up, Mrs. Seams, the wife of a Republican leader, came gushingly in. 'Oh, Mrs. Ellis, we are so happy over your election! Elmer is just too delighted!' And she stopped for breath and to lace her shoes, having left home in a hurry.

So I was elected. She straightened up and went on, 'I wanted to be the first to congratulate you, and Elmer says he will be right down and help you choose your deputy.'

'But, Mrs. Seams,' I said, 'I've already chosen my deputy.' This, to use the words of my son, who had by now joined us and stood taking it all in, 'knocked her ears back.' She left.

Earl and I ran to talk it over with the family, and we were excited and happy — all talking at once. Then I went home and started to clean the house, which had been sadly neglected. A young man, a very fine, well-liked college graduate — the only son of one of the prominent bankers — came and asked to be my deputy. This, I don't know why, more than anything else, opened my eyes to the fact that there was more to the job of being treasurer than I had realized. It hurt me when I had to tell him it was promised, and I began to wonder if I had been foolish in asking Jean. Still, I knew if I had not done so I should not have had the small majority which had elected me.

It was not long until others came, trying to get me to change; telling me frankly that neither of us knew enough to run the office. I said, 'We can learn.' They said, 'Jean isn't even a Republican.' I said, 'Oh, yes, she is. You ask her.' (When I had asked her to be my deputy, we decided that she was a Republican.)

I didn't get any house-cleaning done. All day my porch was a battle-ground. I would not give in. Oh, it is sweet to feel power for the first time!

Haranguing men told me what I could and could not do; and right there, I commenced to see clay feet and they commenced to see a new Annie Ellis. I think men down town were betting whether she would or would not stand pat. I did stand pat, thereby spilling political beans and making enemies from the jump.

After a few days things, as far as I was concerned, commenced to simmer down. I knew, however, that there was plenty of talk and speculation. 'A cook in the Court-House!

What will a cook do in the Court-House?'
And the after-election post-mortems! — how
entertaining, amusing, and, yes, instructive.
Here is one: In Bonanza, my sister Jose, weeks
before election, had been very kind to a hard-
shelled Democrat. She had baked numerous
cakes and pies and given them to him, on each
trip electioneering for me, until she thought
she had his vote cinched.

As it happened, they were both on the election board and, when they were counting, Jose
crackled a vote and threw up her head, rather
out of humor (I wasn't running very well);
looked at her before-election Democratic friend,
and remarked, 'I thought you said, when I
took you that last spice cake, that you would
vote for Annie?' The poor man was startled,
and stammered, low-voiced, 'Why — why I
did.' Jose, madder than ever, said, 'Like fun
you did! Just look at that!' and she threw the
ballot at him. (Don't ask me how she knew it
— she's clever.) The poor man did look at it,
and said meekly, 'Well, I do declare, my hand
must have slipped.'

Before election there was one precinct I did
not visit. It is high in the mountains with
only seventeen, or twenty votes there, at best.
Election day was so stormy and the snow was

so deep that only a few of those people could get to the polls, four or five men and one woman. I had known her slightly. They raised cattle and sheep on their high mountain ranch, and all day while she herded sheep, her fingers were busy with the most fairy-like, cobwebby lace. She worked like a man and a woman, too. I've heard of her taking newborn wet lambs from her oven and slipping a pan of biscuits in, and *vice versa*. I heard that on election day she fought every step of the way trying to force her horse through the storm; then she got off, and, breaking the track, led him until she reached the voting place, wet and tired. Then she voted and returned home again. I thought this wonderful, and later, when she came to town to pay her taxes, I told her so. I told her also how I appreciated the fact that she would get out and fight through the storm in order to vote for me. She looked at me with the clear, far-seeing eyes of the people who live in high places, and said, 'Yes, it was a bad day and a hard trip — but I didn't vote for you.'

CHAPTER X

I would trust my virtue, my pocketbook, or my life to a man
whom I would not trust in politics — because in politics, no
man is free.

A. E.

Of course there were storms and storms; but I
heard only a few, as I was busy getting my
house in order and making over my clothes. I
did not get any new ones because, with the as-
surance of two years' work at eighteen hundred
dollars a year, I could see looming up in the far
future college for my son.

As I sewed, secretly I tried to teach myself
some things that I thought would help. First,
I was very forgetful and could not concentrate.
I got Kipling's poem 'If' — determined to
learn it. I found this was a job, but after a
struggle, repeating it at night when lying
awake, I finally mastered it. I thought that
since I was to handle money, it might be well
to brush up a bit on my arithmetic; so I hunted
out an old Ray's Arithmetic, with its yellow
back and its frightening, elusive insides. I
tried to figure out parts of it, but I couldn't; it
tortured me just as it did when I was a child;
there were the same multiplication tables as

then — the friendly twos and fives, the harder threes, fours, sixes, and the never-could-be-learned sevens and nines. The tens and elevens looked as though I might manage them, but I never got that far, and I had a sinking of heart and stomach when I came to a page of miscellaneous examples. Then I asked the friendly Assessor what I could learn to help me. He advised reading the law on taxes and on the collection of taxes. I tried it hard — the longer I read, the less I knew.

Now, there was talk of my not being able to get a bond. Boss M—— came to me and offered, through his bank, to furnish my bond. I wouldn't agree to that, as I didn't want to be obligated to any one. I was going it blind without advice or guidance; laughing when I heard criticism of my ability to run the office, because, no matter what they said, they did not know the half of it.

Then I, without weighing it especially, did this unheard-of, unusual thing. How they all must have laughed — both Republicans and Democrats; some openly, some in chagrin, some in their sleeves. I laugh now when I think of it. In town there were several agents for bonding companies — two of them Republicans; one was a very good friend of mine to whom I should have given it. Another was Elmer, who expected me to give it to him; another was my Democratic opponent whom I had just beaten in the election. I suppose I felt a little sorry for him; then, too, I wanted him friendly, hoping he would teach me the office work. Anyway, I asked him to get my bond for me — how startled and surprised he must have been, but he never turned a hair! It meant a hundred dollars to him. I wish it were all to do over again, because probably I'd do the same again, except now I should watch and enjoy their actions and reactions. I imagine I was getting a reputation as an iconoclast — only they would call it 'damned fool.' However, I never heard anything, because when some one started to tell me anything not to my credit, I cut him off at the pockets, letting him know I had less use for the repeater than for the original oracle.

The bonding house sent a man down from Denver to look me over. I suppose it was hard for the local agent, being a sincere and honest Democrat, to recommend me for a seventy-five-thousand-dollar bond — fifty as Treasurer, twenty-five as Public Trustee. I wonder just what he did say, so as not to commit himself and still to get that one hundred dollars, not being able to praise his successor and certainly not being able to run her down. And to think I had always lived so entirely within myself that there was no one for me to laugh with! The Denver representative came to see me in my own home that I had built bit by bit. We talked of many things; I told him the truth — that there was no money back of me; that I knew nothing of business, but that he could depend on my honesty. When he left, it made me very happy to have him say that he would report to the bonding company that they would be safe in bonding me to any amount.

Mr. Sloan, as had often been the custom, did not invite me into his office to learn. At first I blamed him; later, I found it would have been impossible for him to have me there, and that the only way to learn the work was to do it; and if one were there for years, each day one would have something new and different to learn. The Assessor did let Jean and me go into his office, where we filled in and directed the tax cards to be sent January the first. All were signed with my name. I felt important and business-like; it was lucky I couldn't see into the future. One day the banker came from Center. This man was one of the directors of the shearing plant, and knew that a few months before I could not, unaided, make out the men's board bill; now he was willing and anxious to turn over to me the handling and custody of money which in a year's time amounted to many millions of dollars. He called me to one side; it seemed he wanted, after all he'd done for me, some kind of a promise about the bank deposits. While standing there talking to him, my thoughts and speech having no connection — they so often don't — the Assessor passed me and went into the vault. I could see him, but no one else could. He shook his head at me, and all that time I was laughing and talking. Then he wrote on a large piece of paper, 'Promise nothing. Tell him to meet with the other bankers and decide among themselves.' This I did, and got credit for good judgment.

On January the first, I took over the office, and was sworn in. My predecessor turned over the keys and gave me checks for the county money. We were off, watched hopefully by a few, critically by many.

Can you imagine a woman, who knew only a sewing machine and an egg-beater, almost in an hour turning to adding machine, typewriter, and calculating machine? A woman to whom a seventy-five-dollar check was big money now handling millions; a woman who had never had a banking account, who did not know how to make out a check properly, now doing daily business and having checking accounts on five different banks? I can't tell you how little I did know then; you would not believe it, or that men who did know would permit it. Oh, from politics I 'learned about men.'

I found that in preparation the things that would have helped me most were for me to have known my A B C's readily, backward and forward; and to have learned how to make change; also to have learned the descriptions and the divisions of land.

It was a frightful fighting time, filled with books and books and more books. The large vault was lined from top to bottom with huge, heavy record books, many of which took both Jean and me to lift. It was appalling. I at once invented a sort of a tea-wagon affair, and that saved us somewhat. The strain was awful. Many a time have I gone into the vault and, to keep the tears back, bitten my lips until I tasted blood. We worked after hours, nights, Sundays, and holidays, trying to get through the mountains of mail. Each letter contained money and pertained to matters we knew nothing of. Books — books — fund and cash books, rolls, and receipt books for each year — all looking alike to a beginner, but very different, we found to our sorrow. There were tax certificates and certificates of taxes, which sound alike and aren't; warrants, thousands of warrants of many different kinds, which could be so easily mixed — and were.

How we worked! How we had to work! Many times have I been struggling, trying to make an extension on a given description of land; or figuring interest for and in front of a banker; and in my desperation have gone into the vault and rattled papers with one hand and wiped tears with the other.

At this stage of the game, I changed my name Annie to Anne, just to gain the time lost in dotting that 'i.' Even that much more time seemed to help.

The Assessor and his deputy were very helpful so far as they could be, but no one knew how the books were kept. A bookkeeper from one of the stores came and offered to help, but when he found we carried our credits and disbursements directly opposite to the way he was accustomed to do it, he left in disgust. A former treasurer offered advice, but when he had had the office, all of his adding was done by hand and head; now there were two adding machines going full tilt; a woman who had been deputy years before was kind enough to come for a few days and make receipts, and I hired, with my own money, the man who had the abstract office to help for a short time.

I thought I knew what work was, but this was the worst I'd ever been up against. We were in the office at eight in the morning, and on our feet all day, lifting those heavy books seemingly every minute of the time. It was a constant strain trying to concentrate on the job in hand while hearing conversations, click of typewriters, the grind of the Marchant calculator, and the snap of the adding machines. There is no privacy in a public office as there is in a bank, and the work is just as hard. Often, when we were answering very important mail and only part-way through a job, several people would come into the office, each wanting something different — as important (more so because a taxpayer in person is also a voter) and as hard as the job we had left unfinished, and as liable to error, which in a Treasurer's office cannot, must not be.

Each day we worried; realizing the need of a daily balance and not knowing how to make one; sometimes in our rush hanging up a check without making a receipt for it. (This was done with a very large check which, if I had been dishonest, I could have kept and it never would have been found out.)

We tried several plans, none of which worked; then, after the State Auditors came, they showed me a way which was really very simple — I mean, when it worked. I found business men very patient and helpful. One of our pioneers, from butcher shop to banker, and considered crabbed, took time to tell me that to date a document or paper was important and must be done.

I did a great deal of work for George Corlett, Colorado's present Lieutenant-Governor; he always made his own legal papers and every detail was made so plain that it was almost impossible to err; then, when I sent the finished work to him, he would write, 'I have received so and so, which *seems* correct.' This I thought clever. I remember that when the Colorado Fuel and Iron Company sent a check in payment of their taxes, which ran into thousands of dollars, I made an error of three dollars in their favor, and Fred Farrar, their secretary, wrote me many letters patiently and pleasantly trying to get it straight.

That first month was a horror of work and worry. It was days before I could master the combination to the vault without the paper; finally one noon I decided to end it. I did not go home to dinner; instead I pulled a chair in front of that door and turned and twisted, opened and shut it until I could do it; then, to burn my bridges, I burned the paper. A good thing, too, as soon after this a playful fool shut the vault door on Jean, and I, without loss of time — calm outwardly, raging inside — released her.

I used to wake in the night worrying over the work, then would come the fear that we had not put all the books away or that I had left the vault open. Sometimes this feeling would be so strong that I would get up and go to the Court-House — to find everything all right. One night there was an alarm of fire and without being fully awake I ran for the Court-House.

Then — and this was tragedy — I lost the Court-House keys. Now there might be some excuse for my other mistakes, but any fool ought to be able to keep track of a bunch of keys.

Both Jean and I had keys; she carried hers on a string around her neck and used to come to the door with her arms full of mail, fish in the front of her dress, then bend herself double and open the door. This didn't look business-like enough for me, so I put my keys on a clip, hooked it over my belt — and lost the whole works; also weight, and appetite, and sleep. For a week, Jean, every time we opened the door, tied herself into a knot; at last some one found my keys.

When we tried to make the first month's reports for the state, the county, the commissioners, and the schools — and it was work, grueling work; and when the bank statements came in, and we found we were short thirteen hundred dollars — all this about polished us off. We searched and hunted; going through receipts, disbursements, and warrants, time and time again. Before this in a smart-alecky way I had said, 'Sometime I would like to go to prison, because there I could rest and read and invite my soul.' When this money could not be found — search as we might, and fearing that in our hurry and confusion we might have burned a check, I saw looming up a possibility that I might have a chance to cool my heels in Cañon City.

At this time came the successful candidates' dance — the irony of it. Jean had stood faithfully by during these hectic days, although I think she was sick of her job and would have thrown up the sponge if I had weakened in the least — which I didn't, not in public; what I did in private was nobody's business.

This dance was just too much, and we decided not to go. In our search for the lost money, we had reached a point where we were doing foolish things, such as calling the janitor, a melancholy man. We asked him if he had seen any check in the waste-paper basket. He was peeved — his natural state — and said, 'What 'ud checks be doing in the waste-paper basket?' — and what would they, I'd like to know? He went on, sadly and disgustedly, 'I did find one left on the desk one night.' I burned with shame. I knew he did, and I was the guilty one.

The Assessor was by this time helping us look for the lost funds; and he overheard us say we were not going to any dance — not with that hanging over us, and with the reports to get ready for the County Commissioners. He was a good politician and said, 'This is no stage in the game to quit; of course, you will go to the dance. That money's somewhere.' And we did go, and the next day we discovered that the money had been deposited in the bank to pay interest on bonds, but did not show on the monthly statement.

After a time the work lessened and we learned something about the business so that it became less of a nightmare. With the exception of a small group of men, all of whom were in my own party, people helped me in every way possible. These men, when I first went into office, were very gracious — unduly so — offering advice and almost telling me each move to make; they were especially urgent and helpful about my deposits in a certain bank. At first they almost patted me on the back, almost as if to say, 'Nice Annie — good politician; she knows her way about; she's going to give us the biggest end of the deposits.' But she didn't. Then they tried to bribe me — that is, if you'd consider the promise, only, of a box of candy a bribe. Well, I didn't get the candy.

Then they tried to force me — that is, if you would call forcing never coming into the

office without a sneer on their lips and a chip
on every shoulder. My deputy would say,
'How can you stand it? Why do you stand it?'

These men, who were supposed to be my
friends, tried to make it hell for me; but I,
who recognize no hell, was neither worried,
frightened, nor disturbed; in fact, I rather enjoyed it; holding the whiphand was to me a
new experience. One of these men was later
Treasurer in this same office and recently,
after leaving a large shortage behind him,
died by his own hand.

In my office, if there were any favors shown,
it was to the poor taxpayer who handed me,
with his work-gnarled, rusty hands, money
saved bit by bit; some silver, and soiled checks
for small amounts — the balance made up by
his own carefully written check. He would
stop me when I asked about the potato crop
and ask me to make the interest as small as
possible, often almost pleading with me not to
sell his land; and though it's against the law,
also against the wishes of many, I ignored several tax sales. To foreclose on any man's land
was the thing I hated most; next to that was to
give a Treasurer's tax deed. While I was in the
office came the after-war slump, and I had
many foreclosures, among them the ranch and

home of my best friends, and they will never know how it hurt me to have to do my duty.

Years before this, there had been in our county an opening or sale of land which was a graft from the time that the gullible 'Oklahomians' bought it after seeing pictures of fruit trees weighed down with fruit. Those five-acre tracts made more work and caused more grief than anything else in the office. Many times I have written letters to complaining taxpayers who had lost their land — lawfully but not rightfully; and when I signed the letter, 'Yours truly,' I felt ashamed. One such letter, sent to the poet Edmund Vance Cooke, brought forth a red-hot answer. He said we were all a bunch of crooks, the Treasurer the worst of the lot; that we were barking up the wrong tree, and that we'd better do something about it or he would. No, those aren't Edmund Vance's words, they are mine. What he said was:

'I have regularly received all sorts of communications... which have been well calculated to make one believe that the land-dealers, landowners, lease-holders, county and town and state officials, and the general population of Colorado is composed of a race of deadbeats and unhung rascals generally.'

[173]

Now, Edmund Vance, in spite of being a poet, knew his taxes, and there was something done about it. When I wrote him, I explained that there might be rascals in office, but that as near as I could I was doing my best; and I asked him, since he was so bright (I didn't like that 'deadbeat' word), how he happened, in the first place, to have been stung with one of those tracts. When he answered what he called my 'human letter,' he enclosed one of his poems published in the 'Saturday Evening Post,' entitled, 'I Had a Friend.'

Women who do office work and also their housework, do too much. All the week I worked in the office; and on Sunday, pulled in the old tin tub and bathed; then washed my hair; then I also washed and ironed some clothes; cleaned the house; and cooked for the following week; also mended and cleaned our clothes. Earl was in High School and helped all he could, after practicing each night during the football, basketball, and track seasons. I found, each month, that after all, one hundred and fifty dollars did not go so very far, and that I must save almost as closely as I ever had. I did branch out and subscribed for the 'Denver Post,' the 'Literary Digest,' and the 'Saturday Evening Post.'

I bought a Bible and a dictionary and an old set of Barrie's books, 'Main Street,' and Roosevelt's letters to his children. It seemed lovely to buy books.

Jean proved that in my selection of her I had shown great wisdom; she was a tireless worker, strong, faithful, and efficient, and, best of all, knew enough to keep her mouth shut; if any news ever leaked from the office, it was the Treasurer who talked. At the end of two years, when I must again get out and make the campaign for reëlection, Jean carried on the work alone, because — which I think absurd — the public, which expects you to spare no effort in order to hold your job, would be the first to criticize if you should put some one in your place while doing it.

My opponent this time was a woman — a well-educated, worth-while person. The worst thing against her was that she was married and in politics a husband is not an asset.

All campaigns are very much alike. In my favor this time was the fact that I could run and had run the office without help or interference from any political gang.

I now remember only a few incidents of that campaign. It was the year in which Harding ran against Wilson for the Presidency. One

Sunday I went walking with two cultured and intelligent women. One was a banker's wife who I hoped would vote for me; the other a professor's wife, a staunch Democrat, and I feared, while she liked and admired me, that she would not vote for me. After a while we rested, sitting in the warm sun. I drew designs on the ground with a stick and listened to those two women talk. The banker's wife said she had had a letter from a cousin who lived in Washington and some one had told her that President Wilson was not a moral man. The professor's wife was shocked, and said in that case she would have to vote for Harding. I was glad because I knew, if she scratched for the President, she would for me. Poor thing, wouldn't she be disappointed when she heard of 'The President's Daughter'? Some Presidents lead one to wonder if even 'Cal is cool.'

CHAPTER XI

When any one tells you that you are a superior person, keep your feet on the ground, and your hand on your pocketbook, your vote, or what have you.

A. E.

THE second campaign was much the same as the first one; going over the whole county electioneering; that is, going when we were not broken down. I have been broken down in dust, in mud-holes, on hillsides, in hollows, and in hot sunshine, in snow, in rain, and in sleet; and I found that, with a cheerful disposition and a stiff upper lip, one can make many friends, and thereby votes, among the innocent bystanders who gather to aid or to advise.

One time in particular it seemed as though the car never would go again. The young woman who was running for County Superintendent of Schools was with me. At the beginning of the campaign in the middle of a committee meeting, she started to leave, and some one told her that that just wasn't done; but she went on, flinging over her shoulder, 'Damned if I'm going to stay here and choke on tobacco smoke!' I thought, 'Old girl, if you can't stand more than that, politics is no place for you.' But she fooled me; in the hard campaign she was tireless, and later I learned, fearless, with two feet of her own which she stood on. One day we walked for a mile up the dusty road, then crawled through a barbed-wire fence and went over a ploughed field to a little house squatting inside a broken-down fence, the gate of which was the foot of a white iron bed wired to a post. Everything was run down, showing shiftlessness, poor management, and poverty; but no filth. Several dogs ran at us snarling and barking. I went forward, fearlessly outside, but trembling inside. I'm afraid of dogs, but I pretend I'm not. I said aloud, 'Nice doggie, good fellow' (never hit a prospective voter's dog). I tried to catch his eye. This never had worked, but it might, and then I hissed low, 'Get out or I'll knock the daylights out of you, you ugly beast!' and muttered to my companion, 'The poorer people are, the more darned dogs they have.'

Then the door was opened by a woman with troubled eyes and mouth. She was pulling together her waist, which was old in style and in material.

At once I sensed we should not be there, we were not wanted. We were embarrassing this woman, who, by now, in a beautiful educated

voice had asked us in. There seemed to be but
one room with a lean-to on one side, rough
planks for the walls, with cracks between the
boards that a cat could and did walk through.
I was at a loss for words. I could not, in the
face of the woman's poverty, pride, distress,
and misery, talk of mere politics. I wanted to
put her at her ease. I had suffered in my time
just as she was suffering now. I can't tell you
what she looked like; all I saw was her hands
fluttering — first at her hair, then at her waist
front, then rolling and unrolling her sleeves;
fluttering hands and hurt eyes. Then, a noise.
I looked up, and almost cried, 'Have you a
baby?' In an instant everything was changed;
her eyes brightened; she smiled; the fluttering
hands were eagerly clasped; she said, 'Yes,
come and see him.' All her shame and embarrassment were gone. Here was a treasure she
was proud and happy to display. She led us
into the low lean-to room — it was airless and
smothering hot; she pulled away the mosquito
netting which she had used to keep away the
swarming flies — and there was the child.

We gathered around the bed, the proud
young mother, the girl who had never been a
mother, and I, a mother and grandmother;
and, smiling down at this sleeping baby, we

were drawn together, and politics seemed trivial and a long way off. When I left, as I swung
the bedstead gate, it was almost reverently.

Never did I say anything harmful of my opponents. In the first place, I knew nothing,
because always they were the strongest and
best candidates on the opposite ticket. In the
second place, I found that it was poor policy;
because the moment you start to criticize your
opponent, the person you are talking to naturally commences to look for your glass house;
so, on the contrary, I always praised whoever
was running against me.

A day would go something like this: After I
had climbed out of the car for the hundredth
time, reached for my cards and shaken my
clothes down — very tired, but knowing I
must not miss a place — and had managed to
open the gate (I'll bet I've opened more gates
than any other woman in Saguache County,
each with a different fastening, too), and had
run the gantlet of barking dogs, the door would
be opened by a resentful woman with an air
of, 'You're not going to talk me over.'

I would tell her who I was and what I
wanted, and she, with a chip on her shoulder
attitude, would say, 'The woman who is run-

ning against you was here yesterday and seems very nice.' I always returned, 'I should say she was nice, and capable' (so was I); 'so honest' (none honester than I), 'and such a rustler' (if this woman had ever heard of me at all, she would know that I was a rustler), 'and so efficient' (the first time I ran I left the word 'efficient' strictly alone); and I would continue, 'If she is elected, she will make just as good an official as I will, only I need it, and I don't want her to have my job.' Then the woman would say, 'Well, you know, I like to hear you talk like that' — and I had won a vote — maybe. This is one thing I have learned from politics — don't rant. The man you are ranting against today, you may, at the next election, have to ask a favor of. The best thing is to 'lay low' and keep them guessing.

On this trip, at the dance in Bonanza, I was dancing with one of the bosses from the Rawley mine, and he asked me what I thought of prohibition. I beat around the bush, since politics, prohibition, and religion are things I discuss with no prospective voter. He went on and told me that, in order to hold the men and run the mine, 'They just have to have booze,' otherwise the men would be dissatisfied and go where they could get it.

Every campaign is much like another —
rush and rush. I remember one day I wanted
extra cards, and almost ran to the printer,
flung his door open, and called to some one I
heard in the room, 'Print me three hundred
cards.' He yelled back, 'What do you want
on 'em?' and I, who didn't want 'Mrs.' on
them, called out, 'Plain Anne Ellis,' and when
he delivered the cards they were printed:

PLAIN ANNE ELLIS

Candidate for County Treasurer
Republican Ticket

Again I was elected; and in our county ran
ahead of every one on the ticket including
President Harding.

A few days after the election, several politicians and influential persons were gathered in
my office, telling how it all happened and doing
quite a lot of Babbitt bragging. Elmer, who
felt his political oats, and tried to look states-
manlike by closing his teeth and drawing his
lips sternly down, said, 'But I don't see how
Mrs. Ellis does it.' Then he laughed — some
people do when they knife you — 'It must be
all the Mexicans she's cooked for.' I looked
him in the eye and said calmly, 'Elmer, you

mean that for a slam, but I think it's a compliment.' His neck reddened in anger. Some people's do.

The time passed quickly — it does when you're busy. My son was nearing the end of his High School work. We led a very quiet life, only going occasionally to a picture show; he, of course, went to many of the dances, and I went to some parties. Jean and I took turns about going, as we were both invited; I would never consider that she was working for me, only that we were partners, which we were. Just a few days ago I wore to the Arizona Biltmore a dress that I made by hand, evenings, ten years ago, when we were sitting at home, Earl getting his lessons, I dreaming and sewing and planning that Earl should go to college. So far as I knew, none of Earl's father's people nor mine had been to college. How we talked it over! I was more eager than he, and had utterly different views from his. With him it was football; with me, a symbol of what I hoped we might be; that we might reach a place where, instead of being job-hunters, we could be job-givers. I believe that this is the power behind most endeavor — wanting for our children what we have wanted and have been denied.

Somewhere about this time the Women's League of Equal Rights was having a convention and a big pageant in the Garden of the Gods at Colorado Springs. I was invited, and, while I knew it would be expensive, I decided to have a fling and go. I called Neita, who lived near Denver, and suggested that she join me. She wanted to, but could not afford it any better than I, so we gave it up.

Then she called me late at night. 'This always saving gets monotonous, let's go.' I sat up the rest of the night finishing a lace dress that I wished to take. I had a very good suit and blouse — costing seventy-nine dollars, to be exact; much the best thing I'd ever owned. In Salida I bought me a hat and was all set — or so I thought; but I got into Colorado Springs before Neita did, and when she was stepping off the train she said, 'Where did you get the sombrero?' So the first thing I did was to buy a new hat.

We stayed at the Antlers Hotel; in fact, we were 'going the whole hog.' Mrs. O. H. P. Belmont, who was head of this movement, gave a luncheon at the Broadmoor Hotel. Neita and I were invited. I was thrilled inside; outside I was trying to act 'to the manner born.' I sat next to Nellie Burget Miller, poet laureate of Colorado; and visited with her, the while taking mental recipes of every dish served. (I can do this.) I complimented her on her answer to a criticism about her work which had been published in the 'Literary Digest'; she thanked me and told me it was a long time before she could write again, because, she said, she was like a robin which had been singing and, having had stones thrown at it, was not apt to sing soon again.

Governor Sweet spoke at this convention, also former Governor Shoup, and I met and talked to both. It reminded me of another Governor whom I had met a year or so before. It was at Cattleman's Day in Gunnison, and I had watched all the bucking, the horse-racing and the bull-dogging events, and had gone outside to sit in the car of the friend who had brought me. I climbed into the front seat, as there was a stranger in the back. As I got in, I said, 'The Governor is going to speak, and I came out here to rest.' He replied, 'I suppose listening to a Governor is a bore to most people; I know it is to me'; and he started to leave. 'Anyway,' he continued, 'I believe I shall go and hear him.' After he left, I thought, 'If he can stand it I can,' and I followed. You've guessed it — he was the Governor.

I enjoyed every minute of Mrs. Belmont's luncheon, the food was lovely, and, as I ate, I planned how I would bring into future conversations, 'The time I had luncheon with Mrs. O. H. P. Belmont at the Broadmoor.'

We went out to the Garden of the Gods to help with the pageant. There were hundreds already there — Alice Paul standing on the hillside like another Napoleon, directing and commanding, changing her orders before one had a chance to carry them out. I would say, at a snap judgment, that she has the big-head. I heard a woman from New York, who was some kind of a leader, say: 'She [Alice P.] always mixes things up. We were both on the committee which met President Wilson on his return from Europe' — and I didn't get just what it was, but whatever it was, Alice was blamed. That day in the pageant (a miracle of wonder to me) were marching women dressed in white, hundreds of marching women. At a certain stage of the game, Alice Paul decided they were to be given tin cups which were to be passed through the crowd for donations. Then she changed her mind, and, I suppose, thought all the women should know it instantly; anyway, a number went on passing the can, and Alice lashed out at them with her tongue — at this she was good. All day I did not see her smile. Poor thing! I think she wasn't well!; probably while she was working for equal rights for women, nature was having its way with her and demonstrating the main reason why it is almost impossible for women to take their place beside men.

That night we went to a reception at Mrs. Spencer Penrose's. I had had no chance to wear my lace dress, so there I did, and found every one else in suits and hats. Anyway, I handed my cape to the maid, the first capped and aproned maid I had ever seen, and went boldly in, hoping people would think me a house guest or something. In spite of knowing I was wrongly dressed, which is not an especially comfortable feeling, I enjoyed it immensely.

Naturally, during this meeting Susan B. Anthony and Elizabeth Cady Stanton were frequently eulogized. Now, long years before this, when these two women were touring the West in the cause of women's rights, they had spoken in Saguache and stayed all night. Mother Ellis, who was one of the first pioneers, had heard them and had told me all about it — how they were dressed, what they said, and how they were received. At the Colorado

Springs meeting, neither Neita nor I kept this a secret.

I remember going up to Neita, who, distinguished in gray lace, with her yellow hair piled high on her head, was the center of a group of women, one of whom was Sue White, the militant picketer. She had been in prison, and wore, to prove it, a large pin representing prison bars, with lock, chains, and everything. Only those who had been in jail had the right to wear such a decoration. Sue was a persuasive talker and was soliciting money, and I think, when I rescued her, Neita was being urged to contribute a thousand dollars to the cause.

The next morning we left for home. I saw Neita off, then went to my own train, on which, as it happened, Mrs. Belmont and her crowd were leaving. They had a meeting at the station. I knew only Alice Paul, Mrs. Belmont, and Mrs. Shoup, who was by far the best-dressed woman there. Mrs. Belmont seemed tired, old and disillusioned. I got the idea that the others thought they were working her. They weren't; she's clever. Alice Paul talked. This, I believe, is her forte. All the other women seemed to consider her wonderful; I might have, too, if I hadn't seen her lose her temper.

Again they were raising money. This time it was to send a woman speaker over Colorado. A woman was chosen from this group — she was to get two hundred dollars per month, and, as far as I knew, was the only one, financially, who gained from that equal-rights-for-women meeting.

CHAPTER XII

When any one repeats to me something that has been said about me — unless it's complimentary — I take the starch out of the first speaker, also out of the repeater, by saying, 'Is that all? Thank God, they don't know what I do.'

A. E.

WHEN my term of office was over, I decided not to run again. There is no future in politics. It costs about all one can save to make a campaign every two years.

Before this I could say, like the cowboy, 'My money don't cost me nothin'; I work for it.' I found that in politics you worked for it, hard; and, besides, it cost you something — something of your self-respect and a lost faith in mankind.

Months before, I told every one I was not going to run, that I positively would not run. On the day they were to make the nominations, I left the office and the town. I didn't want to be argued with. On my return that evening, I found five men waiting on my porch — five of the most influential men in the county. They told me I had been drafted and must run. Then in turn they talked. Boss M—— said, 'You have made one of the best officials we've ever had.' Another said, 'You are the strongest

[190]

candidate on the entire ticket.' Still another, 'You owe it to the party' (somehow an official is always in debt to his party). Then the County Attorney spoke; he had been very wonderful to me; besides, he knew his arguments. 'It seems foolish to throw up the office at this time; I don't imagine you have saved money and you have started Earl to college. I know this has been your life's ambition and it will take money — much more than you can earn in any other way.' I weakened; he knew I would, and I cried out, 'But you know I can't run against Alta.'

Alta was the deputy assessor, a fine girl, honest and efficient, who, in my struggle to learn the office work, had done everything in her power to help me. I liked and admired her very much, as she did me. Now I had grown to love the office — I mean the work and the service to the taxpayers and I wanted to leave it in good hands. My deputy would have been wonderful, only she would have nothing to do with politics. Alta was the logical person — no, not logical, because she was an ardent Democrat; when I insisted I would not run, she was nominated on the Democratic ticket, and I was glad.

Those men urging me to run knew that she

would win. I went on, 'You know Alta never would have accepted the nomination had she known that I would run.' Then Boss M——— said, 'You will not be running against her, because she'll never qualify. Come on, Sister, and run.' It was late in the evening. Inside the door I could hear my family listening and I knew praying that I would accept — and I did. Then the men left me — not quite in tears, but almost.

I went in, washed myself, and changed my clothes. I felt soiled — felt that I had done something to be ashamed of. Then, although it was far into the night, I went to Alta's. There was no emotion on either side, although both our souls and hearts were stripped bare. Quietly, though with clenched hands, my throat hurting, so the words would hardly come, I told her I was going to run; quietly she said, 'Yes, I heard that you were.'

This was killing me; still quietly I said, 'And you know, Alta, when I go, I go to win.' Oh, why didn't she say she would not run? Instead, in a flat voice, she answered, 'Yes, I know.' She wasn't the kind to quit. No more was said, only for once, instead of being flippant, I was melodramatic, and said as I closed the door, 'God pity us both.'

And so the race was on. We were about equal in strength, and never during the campaign did either of us say an ill thing of the other. In fact, I heard that at a Democratic meeting, when a speaker said something not to my credit, Alta jumped to her feet and said it wasn't true.

Prior to this I had had as Public Trustee a foreclosure involving thousands of dollars and many people, all of whom, as it happened, were Republicans. In this foreclosure there were wheels within wheels — of business, politics, and social prestige; the whole affair was egged on by a foolish, futile, family feud. In the final settlement of this affair, I had the power of decision, and, as I knew little about law, I did what I thought right (many of my decisions were quite Sancho-Panza-ish). Elmer was the lawyer on one side, and naturally expected me to do as he wished. I didn't. He threatened me politically. I laughed, and we went round and round; then he threatened me with a writ of mandamus. I didn't know just what this was, but I knew, if Elmer had a hand in it, it wouldn't be nice; still, I told him to go to it. I decided against his clients, who, to this day, think I was bought. Right here I will write so all who run may read; at no time did one of the people on the side who won ever write or say anything to influence me in any way; they must have given me credit for doing my duty as I saw it, because they never even thanked me; while the other side took it as a personal matter and I lost many Republican votes. When influential families fight among themselves, it is well, if I may use an old expression of my mother's, to 'Hide out, little ones.'

In this election nothing was left unturned that might lose me a vote. For instance, when prohibition went into effect in our State there was a law that permitted each householder to buy so many quarts of bottled goods. And I, who had lived in the time when drinking was a disgrace instead of a social grace, and had been taught temperance, not by prohibiting, but by living and learning, and who had never before in my life bought any liquor, now, as the first fruits of prohibition, purchased four quarts of wine. This was used for Christmas dinners, and one bottle was kept for years to celebrate some great occasion like a wedding — mine, maybe.

This story of my buying wine did not do much harm, however, as people knew me too well.

In that campaign the following was for me a

fortunate happening. In a certain town three
women were giving a very large bridge luncheon and a Republican friend wangled me an
invitation. I went and met many ladies whom
otherwise I should have missed. I enjoyed a
well-cooked and well-served luncheon. And
— this was unusual, because I'm a poor card-
player — I won first prize, and when the hostess gave it to me and announced that I was
running for reëlection, I was very happy.

But, shortly this happened, and then I
wasn't so happy: Alta, my opponent, was in
this same town, and an ardent Republican was
giving a party and a Democratic woman, who
was showing Alta around, called the party
giver and asked to bring a friend with her.
When the Republican hostess (I never could
quite decide if this was brave or foolish — I
know that it was sincere, also unfeeling) found
that her guest was the Democratic candidate,
she frankly told Alta that she couldn't come in.
And only I, who knew how sincere and sensitive Alta was, can know how hurt and humili-
ated she felt, as she, with head held high, went
bravely down the walk.

So it went during the weeks before election;
up early, to bed late, traveling all day, often
when I was tired, dirty, and hungry. I knew I

must push on to see a person, 'Because,' I told myself, 'So-and-So lives here; he is going to vote against you, and you don't know how he will take it, coming at this time of night; anyway, it won't do you any harm.' And, cheerfully and enthusiastically, I did see him. A candidate must every moment be enthusiastic in order to keep his workers on their toes, and in spite of frowns and rebuffs, sit, if asked to, and talk of weather, crops, children, and chickens, but never, never of votes.

Two days before election, the county candidates on both sides, also one or two on the State ticket, met in a very picturesque little mining camp in the mountains. Here there were many doubtful votes, and many long-standing feuds. The Democrats beat us in, and took all the best accommodations — not any too good at that; I went to the home of an un-married woman who was queer and cranky — they're apt to be. Her house had stood ever since the early boom days, and had been added to and taken from until now it looked like something that never was. She herself, her house, and the furniture therein would have delighted an antique hunter. I just left my bag and went on to the dance, which was in full swing. It was upstairs in an unheated, unventilated, dusty room filled with a milling mob of miners and their wives and children, and with nervous politicians having every word, movement, and intention weighed and sized up, with those of their opponents who were present. One had to be pleasant to all, especially to the Democrats; thereby peeving Republican friends.

Oh, it's a game all right! I imagine county politics are State politics; and, yes, national and international politics on a smaller scale. After leaving this dance in a snowstorm, tired and weak and counting my money — electioneering costs a lot — my little wren of a landlady showed me through her parlor, gilded chairs, crocheted tidies, what-nots, footstools, crayon portraits, knick-knacks and jim-cracks, and on into my room, which was a cold cubbyhole with no window except a skylight, or something that had once been one, but which now was covered with snow. I undressed and wrapped my petticoat around my feet and crept into a cold bed, which grew colder. Then I found that at some time the skylight had leaked on the bed, which was directly below it, and I was just thawing out the frozen cover. I got up and dressed, went back to bed, and was tortured till morning. And I had the cour-

age, when I paid for my room, to tell the prospective voter that I had passed a good night.
If a politician isn't a born liar, he will learn to
be one.

The following day we visited ranches, I with
a bad cold; then, without rest, we went to a
Mexican dance in our own town, where we
stayed until about ten o'clock; then we
climbed into an open Ford and drove about
eleven miles to a Mexican town, where there
was a dance which would last all night and until the polls opened in the morning. Here there
were several speeches, made first in English,
then in Mexican. We had supper — everything, of course, furnished by the candidates
— going home along toward morning. It was
so cold that the County Clerk's wife and I huddled down in the bottom of the car along with
the chains and a shovel, and covered ourselves
from head to heels with blankets and robes.

Next morning, election day, found me up
bright and early — well, not so bright. All day
I worked, seeing to it that every vote that I
considered mine got to the polls. In no campaign did I feel sure, as many do, and I felt less
so in this one.

On election night we had a dance where
every one went and waited for the returns. It

is a gruelling affair when one is not winning, and I was not winning; had I been, I should have gone home to bed. I knew I must stay. After awhile I commenced to gain a little, then again I was away down; then we were almost neck and neck; then, with a very small majority, I had won. Elected, and not elated. And going home alone through the dark, passing an open door, and seeing Alta's face, pale and drawn, did not add to my happiness.

I had never worn glasses, but with the close work in the office I now needed them. So the morning after election, while the political storm blew over, I started for Denver to have my eyes fitted. Between Saguache and Villa Grove we met a carload of men. Instantly I thought what to say and how best to electioneer them; then came the thought, one sweetly reassuring thought, 'I don't give a damn who you are, where you're going, or whether you vote or not.'

In Denver I went to a cheap hotel. I would, thinking of all the money I'd spent. People are fools. Think how hard I had worked and the money I had spent for a two-year-job! A hard job at that, only paying eighteen hundred a year. County politics, for an honest man who can do anything else, is, I think, mighty poor business.

Denver was having an Armistice Day parade, and while rushing to Dr. Black's I stopped to view the men marching in slushy snow and rain. Then the better to see, I climbed up into a window of an unfinished building, and, standing there in the damp and cold, a whipping wind put the finishing touches on a sickness which seven years later is still with me.

Home again, after that Denver trip, and working hard to catch up the accumulated business. Just before Christmas came a morning when I could not go to work — the Christmas which I had planned so much on. It would be my son's first time home from college. The Christmas before he had spent with Neita, who lived near Denver. I had made prideful preparations. I had intended having a big family dinner, and my cakes, candy, and salted nuts were all ready, made at night. Women, especially mothers, are dear, sweet fools.

By Christmas I was very sick, with two doctors, a trained nurse, relatives gathering in, and friends bringing flowers, flowers that I had never had before, bunches of roses and violets.

On New Year's Day my son carried me to a car. I could neither stand up, sit up, nor lie down. My sister, her husband, and the doctor and the nurse drove on icy, slippery roads over the pass to Salida, where I could be X-rayed.

They considered me dying. I knew I was, and my daughter was sent for. She came, leaving two small children. The doctor told her there was no chance for me — 'W-e-l-l,' he said, 'if she goes South, there might be, though she will probably die on the train.' Neita had received the telegram while she was having a New Year's dinner. She left the turkey on the platter, the guests around the table, and came without even a suitcase. We took the next outgoing train from Salida. We did not know where — only South. We bought the ticket as far as Albuquerque, hoping to get as far as Phœnix. Before arriving in Albuquerque, I was so bad that Neita stood up in the car and asked if there were any Masons on board, and asked them to arrange for us to get off at Albuquerque. They did, and I was taken off on a stretcher. And, because they thought I had T. B. and could not go to a hotel, one of the trainmen let us have his room.

I will not write here of this sickness; sometime I shall, and call it Asthma Anne; then you can either read it or leave it alone. It was a dreadful time. I would not give up to go to bed, thinking I could gain strength by sitting up; I was so weak that my food had to be cut for me; I ate with one hand while I propped my head up with the other. It was a sick, worried, fear-filled time. And I fought — no one will ever know how I fought. Then Earl, thinking his school and my sickness too expensive, quit and went home, only wiring me after he had done so. This almost finished me, but I stood to my guns and had Neita telegraph, ordering him back. Every one thought me foolish, but whenever did I let people keep me from doing what I thought was best for my children?

I was frantic to get home and into the office, and worried frightfully. And I needn't have, because things were going on splendidly; Jean, who was a power of strength, was doing the work of two, and my friends were helping in every way possible. I didn't realize I had so many friends.

Neita nursed me in a cottage for two months, then had to return to her home. Before leaving, she put me in the Methodist Sanatorium. When the Superintendent, as is customary, asked her what church I belonged to, Neita replied, 'Not any.'

'But,' said the woman, 'hasn't she any convictions?' And Neita replied humorously, 'Certainly. She's a Republican.'

CHAPTER XIII

Why change things? A sow's ear is valuable — to the sow; while a silk purse — at best — is only an ornament.

A. E.

IN April I went back to Saguache to work. Never again, though, was I able to work at my old clip. By November I was again ill and my friends urged me to leave. One woman said she didn't mind my killing myself, only it hurt her too badly to watch me do it. I consented to go to Denver and rest for a time, and I wired Neita to meet me there; this she did, but she never even let me leave the station; instead, she wired the Methodist Sanatorium in Albuquerque to have a cottage prepared and for some one to meet me at the train.

So my good nurse, 'Ma' Allphin met me, and again I stayed until spring. (Oh, it wasn't all as easy as it writes.)

This time I made up my mind to be at home for Easter. So each day, as I slowly gained strength, I crawled out of bed, holding onto the bed, and danced. (I can point my toes and dance when I'm too weak to walk.)

One day I read in the paper that there was to be a women's political meeting at the Franciscan Hotel. This was a new hotel built on the Indian plan, and I wanted to see it. So I got out of bed without letting the nurse know, and dressed and slipped out the back way and took a street car.

It was wonderful to see people — people who talked about something besides sickness, doctors, temperatures, and food.

I met a charming woman wearing the most Indian jewelry I'd ever seen on one person — wearing it well too. She was chairman of the meeting. I was later to learn that Ina Cassidy could and did do everything well.

I enjoyed everything so much that I returned to the Sanatorium, changed my clothes, and went back to town — this time in a taxi. I was getting reckless, but it has turned out to be the wisest move I've ever made.

At the banquet each woman stood and introduced the woman on her right, and it was with a thrill that I heard 'Anne Ellis of Colorado.'

That night I made arrangements to stop in Santa Fé on my way home, and stay with the Cassidys, who took a few paying guests. I will not here go into all that that trip meant to me — the old town, the Indians, the Mexicans, the museums, and the interesting people — the kind of people that I had read of, but had never before met — writers and artists. This was my first time ever to see a good painting (of course, there was 'The Battle of Waterloo'). Here I was right in the midst of it, as Gerald Cassidy is an internationally known painter; also the dearest gentleman I've ever known. Mrs. Cassidy belonged to a writers' club, and while I was there, they met one night at her house. Now I had never seen a writer close-up and would have given almost anything to attend that meeting; but I didn't get a 'look-in'; and when you see a movie in which a peeper sees everything through the keyhole — don't believe it. That night I tried it, and it didn't work. How interesting were their conversations, especially at meal-time; meals cooked by Mary, an expert Mexican cook, and served by Carolita, a sweet Mexican maid. There were open fires kept going by Rafael. Mexicans are more than servants. Mary once told a woman who tried to get her away from Mrs. Cassidy, 'No, I'm her friend and neighbor.'

How I blossomed and talked! — often out of turn, I expect; however, not daring many of the words they so lightly used — words I had met in books and knew the meaning of, but did not know how to pronounce. For instance, I heard and saw Witter Bynner, who with his pleasant ways and fancy vest is more like an old-time bartender than a poet. Maybe I should explain to the new generation that a bartender of my time was an efficient, suave, elegant, gracious gentleman who slathered on the goo in gobs.

One night when we were gathered around the fireplace — I remember so well, it was a Sunday night and we had toast, quince jelly, and hot chocolate with whipped cream — I told of the old mining days in Goldfield, Nevada, and when I finished a particularly pertinent — to me — incident, Mrs. Cassidy, with tears in her eyes and a tremble in her voice, said, 'If you could write that as you tell it, it would be worth while.' I did not pay much attention, as every one in Santa Fé has either a brush or pen in hand — sometimes both. They urged me to try to write, and suggested — since I didn't know the first thing about it — to write it to Mrs. Cassidy in the form of letters. Now I could neither spell, punctuate, nor write a clear sentence, but how I wished I could! — and, being the sort of a person who will try anything once, the very next morning before daylight, I began my story and called it, 'The Life of an Ordinary Woman.' I wrote, then warmed my cold, cramped hands underneath the covers, and wrote again.

The kind of stuff and the way I did it, I found came easy. Mrs. Cassidy was not too enthusiastic over my first sample; still she encouraged me and urged me to go on.

A few days after this, I left, having had the best month in my life; left with a new interest — the most compelling, driving, hopeful, soul-satisfying interest I was and am ever to know.

That summer I was not able to work all day in the office, and every moment of spare time was put in trying to write. Often I thought it good; other times I knew it was worthless. To drag things, long forgotten things, from the attic of your memory, to weigh them, to size them up, wondering if they are worth remembering, then to try to arrange them and get them on paper, is no small job, even for one who knows how to do it.

Mrs. Cassidy did not answer any of the letters for a long time; she is a busy woman, the busiest and most competent woman I've ever known. I was frantic for a word. I wanted to know if I could write, if I were writing. Then I wrote two short sketches and had a girl who worked in the Court-House type them for me.

I told her that a woman I had met in the Sanatorium had written them. I'd rather have been caught at almost anything than at trying to write. People would have known that, along with my health, my mind was going, too. I asked her what she thought of them. She said, 'They sound kinda crazy to me; and think of a woman who had to live the way this one did calling her children Joy and Hope' — Neita's middle name is Hope — 'irony, I call it.'

My spirits dropped. Then she went on, 'Still, you can't tell — I used to go to school with a boy — sort of a goofy guy who wrote; these things are a little like his — crazier, though; and now I often see his stories in the "Saturday Evening Post."' So she did compliment me after all!

Then I sent those sketches to Arthur Brisbane (truly, fools do rush in!), who before this had written me a very friendly letter saying, 'When you were a small girl I wrote scores of editorials advocating woman's suffrage, but all my friends wondered why I insisted on making the paper ridiculous. I am very glad to see part of the result in your name at the top of your official paper. If you come to New York, I should like to see you and learn about conditions in your locality. It isn't necessary, I suppose, to add that I am sufficiently old enough to make this invitation excessively proper.'

This he signed himself. I asked his opinion, and he was good enough to answer; he advised me, if I thought I could write, to send them to magazines and let them judge. This letter was signed by his secretary, and my conclusion from this was that Arthur Brisbane did not consider me a knock-out as a writer.

Still I kept on, I was enjoying it too much to quit.

Then I hunted out some of the children's English books, and the first thing I found was by a man named Arno, who wrote that the writer, like the doctor, or lawyer, has to learn to be one. (No hope for me there!) Sir James Barrie said, 'The beginning and end of all literature is to open the minds of people to beautiful thoughts'— still not much hope for me. And Emerson said, 'To write — you do not learn in college, but on the street and from people.' This sounded more like it. And Christopher Morley said, 'Writing is a way of expressing our thoughts and feelings, and until we learn to think and feel generously, finely, bravely, our writing is not apt to be eloquent.' I wondered. That was a little more hopeful.

Then Mrs. Cassidy wrote and told me that I was doing pretty well; she sent the first chapter of Sherwood Anderson's 'A Story-Teller's Story,' and suggested that I try to copy his style. She might just as well have told me to try for the style of Shakespeare! I was attempting something, which, in my case, had neither style nor rule; something I must work out for myself.

I did send a sample, also ten dollars, to Thomas Uzzell, asking him, in his opinion, what the chances were for my becoming a writer. I told him that with me it wasn't a fad; I expected to make my living at it. He answered (he is evidently an honest man) advising me that if I must live, to do it by some other way than writing — or words to that effect.

Again I was very sick — also very worried. Earl was not going back to school; he thought that he could do better to stay out awhile and work. I felt that he would never return to school, and I thought that all my struggle was lost; that in sight of the goal we were quitting, and I was discouraged and disappointed.

That January, my time of Treasurer was up, and I rented my house and went to Santa Fé, where I planned, after a few weeks when I

should be well enough, to start a tea-room —
I just could not give in that I was a sick woman.

The real reason, though, was that I wanted
to talk writing with Mrs. Cassidy. I had by
now sent her four letters or chapters. I found
her absent in Texas. I stayed in her home, and
Mary and Rafael took care of me. It was a
peaceful time when I was writing, a troubled
time when I counted my money, figuring, 'If
so-and-so costs so much, how long will five hundred dollars last?'

It was cold in Santa Fé and I was wheezing
and choking. In writing now, I pass quickly
over those times which were so filled with
worry — not knowing what to do nor where to
go; too sick to do anything or go anywhere. As
soon as the Cassidys returned, I decided to
visit Ruth, my sister who lived in California.
The name California in my mind spelled
warmth and comfort; but I was getting out of
the frying-pan into the fire, or whatever it is
when you go from cold to colder. I found that
Portola is high in the Sierras and very cold.

Here I lived for a time writing some each
day; my sister not very impressed, thinking a
story of our life was just as well kept to ourselves.

By the middle of February, I was so much worse that I decided to go lower and went to Oroville, which, to me, seemed like fairyland — fairyland, with flowers in the yards and fruit on the trees.

I rented two small rooms in a not very good district and really got down to writing. It seemed I coughed all night — and read and typed all day; and in the evening I went out and stole roses. That was the rose time of my life, and how I reveled in them!

The book was written, typed — a great part of it done in bed — and sent to Mrs. Cassidy before the first of May.

During this time I had a strange adventure — a love adventure. All during my sickness every person I met had offered an asthma cure. I tried each one as it came. At this particular time I was taking whiskey and garlic — a brakeman on the Western Pacific had told my sister that it was a sure cure; oh, I've tried worse and more foolish remedies than that! My sister made me some by breaking garlic into tiny pieces, then dropping them into whiskey. The victim every so often ate a garlic bud and drank a little of the whiskey. It should have cured anything, it was vile enough; it may have been adapted to the brakeman's trouble, but it wasn't to mine.

There was a levee not far from where I lived, and on top of the levee was a path. Here I liked to go and watch the Sacramento River. Never did I see any other woman there, but many men, bums and tramps who lay in the grass and slept on the riverside, where they could not be seen from town; if I met one of them on the path, we always passed each other silently.

One day, after a dose of whiskey and garlic, I was sitting there, gasping for breath and watching the river, thinking, 'If only I had the courage, I'm sure that underneath the water it would be no harder to breathe than it is now.'

I am not bad-looking, and I have a way of wearing my clothes, but by no stretch of imagination have I a face that would launch any ships, so I can only account for what followed by the fact that my hat was pulled far down over my face.

To reach the top of the levee, there were, at intervals, steps; and I usually sat near these steps in case one of the tramps was too drunk. That day I was sitting on the top step watching the river when I heard a car draw up and stop; then a quick run up the steps and a man was standing before me. He was dressed in a well-fitting tan business suit, with brown shoes and a tie to match. At a glance I put him down as a competent business man, safe and sure — as reliable as the Rock of Gibraltar, no sense of humor, taking himself and life seriously, a safe bet. He said, very coolly, 'Is this the way to the sand pit?' Now I wanted to hold him to talk to him; for over two months I had not talked to any one except grocery clerks — oh, the terrible loneliness around us. Still, when I answered, I said, 'How should I know when I'm a stranger here dying with asthma?' He was startled and stammered, 'Beg your pardon I, I——' And I, who wanted him to stay more than anything in the world, stubbornly said, 'Better take it and see.'

But he didn't; instead, he came toward me and, reaching out his hand, helped me to my feet, and said, 'Come for a ride with me and I will show you the country.' I never hesitated a moment, but answered, 'All right, I must go to my room and get my cape.' I was so dazed that I started to walk. He said, 'Get in the car and I will take you.'

The luxury of sinking into those cushions, on the front seat, too! It had always fallen to my lot to sit in the back seat — the guest's seat. When I went in for my cape, I almost ran up the steps that so lately I had crept down.

He asked where to go, and I replied, 'Anywhere.' I was struggling to keep the coughs back. Then, 'What do your people mean by letting a sick girl like you be here alone?' The kindness in his voice and the word 'girl' went to my head as no wine could have done, and as we rode along I exclaimed at the wooded hills, the blossoming shade trees and the roses — roses everywhere; and how I talked — too much, perhaps, but I had been so lonely!

When I stopped for breath, he said, 'It's certainly a pleasure and a change to talk to a girl like you.' 'But, man, I am not a girl. I am probably as old as you.' I knew I was older, but age is something I argue with no one.

Then we came to a side road running through mountains of rocks, that, in man's search for gold, had been dredged from the bottom of the Sacramento River. The road gradually grew worse until there was no road at all, and we were in the trees so near the river that it seemed as though another turn of the wheels would take us in. It was lovely — so peaceful and quiet, with only the lapping of the river to break the stillness.

Then a strong hand is laid over both my hands, lying lifeless in my lap; an arm is around my shoulders, and I am drawn to this man and kissed — and I liked it. Still, I drew away — to have been born in the Victorian era certainly cramps one's style, and I said, 'Why spoil all this?' and against my will, 'I think we had better return to town.' And, strange as it may seem, we did. On the way he invited me to go to dinner with him, and a show afterward. I refused; I wasn't able to go to anything.

Then he asked to come later in the evening. He said, now that he had found me, he had to know me better. Oh, he was quite extravagant in his praises and promises! I told him that he might.

This time when I went in, I did run up the steps, in through the door and straight to the mirror; and I did look — no, not beautiful, nor enticing, and not at all alluring, but young, eager, and, if I do say it as shouldn't, interesting.

To find favor in a man's sight had done more, in an hour's time, than gallons of garlic and whiskey — garlic and whiskey! — drat that brakeman, anyway; and I turned straight to the cupboard and took that devil's brew and dumped it down the sink. As I got my simple supper, I danced; I do when I'm happy; and often, when I'm not — then — I am!

Nowadays, when a woman wants to attract a man she slicks her hair back; in my time it was just the opposite — it was fluffed out more, so I fluffed. I did not change my dress because the one I wore was young-looking. I could do nothing to the room; I can make a home in most any place, but there I met my Waterloo — a tiny rusty stove; sad, drab lace curtains; a dresser, a three-legged stand, and one rocker. The *pièce de résistance* was a chameleon bed, or at night it was a bed; in the daytime — well, I don't know, because I never had the strength to close it; but at night I always turned over easy, fearing it would close itself and me too.

This night, to hide the skeleton effect of this wardrobe masquerading as a bed, I threw across the foot a colorful robe, rearranged my vases of roses, and waited.

I was anxious to see this man again; I wanted to talk to him, to draw him out, to learn who he was, where he lived, what he did, and — I wanted to hear him praise me, flatter me, make love to me. I happily and hopefully waited — and waited.

Seven o'clock, eight o'clock, then nine —
but he never came. And I went to bed thinking of Dorothy Parker's 'All my life I wait
around for some damned man.'

Next morning I wondered if I had dreamed
it all, or if it might not have been a vapor of
garlic and whiskey. Anyway, whatever it was,
I felt better for it, and worked gayly on the
book.

Then, two nights later, as I was sitting reading, there came a knock on my door. Before
opening it, I knew it was he. As he came in, he
explained that the previous evening he had
been detained, and this day had driven over
a hundred miles to be with me; that in his absence he had thought and dreamed of nothing
but me. He put his arm across my shoulders as
a husband would put his arms across the shoulder of his old faithful wife, lovingly, tenderly.

He said, 'Come, we will go for a drive.'
This time we went through town, across the
river and up a hill, then through newly blossoming orange groves. Oroville was below us
decked in her loops of lights.

Now I was going to find out something about
him, even though the love-making was music
to my ears, so I said, 'Tell me the story of
your life.' Simply, he started. 'It will only

take a minute; I was born in the East, coming to California when a small boy; one of a large family, poor; I finished grammar school, then high school, then the state normal. I wanted to go on, but my father had helped me, and now I must help him educate the younger children. So I worked for him a number of years, then I went into the automobile business and have been in it ever since; it is all I know. I married a little girl I had gone to school with, and' (here his voice broke) 'a few years ago she died, leaving me with two children, a boy and a girl. Her people wanted the children, but I wouldn't let them go; and while I make a lot of money, it takes a lot; this year the boy finishes college and the girl high school. I am proud of my children' — and his voice rang. If this man were acting, he had missed his calling and, instead of being in business, he should have been on the stage. After a while he drew the car to the side of the road, stopped it, turned off the lights, then gathered me in his arms. I didn't like this — it seemed too cheap, and I told him so.

He laughed indulgently and said, 'You just say that, all women should be and want to be loved.'

'Yes,' I answered, 'poor fools, that is what

leads to their undoing.' And I almost cried
out to him, 'Oh, I know I am old-fashioned;
but this cheapens one so, and while I have
never cared much for other people's opinion,
I have always lived so that I might be proud of
myself. In this world a good many things have
been denied me, but there is one thing I can
have and hold on to, and that is self-respect;
oh, you could never understand.'

He replied, almost tenderly, 'I'm afraid not,
dear.' That word—'dear.' In all my life no
one had called me 'dear,' and how I had wished
some one would! To hear it started an upheaval in my soul, but I simply said, 'I like
that word "dear"' — and he answered, just as
simply, 'That is what I call all the people I
love, my wife, my little girl, and now you.'
We were almost home, and I asked him why
he had not married before this. He answered, 'I have been too busy educating my
children — and I have found no one like
you.'

We were again in my room, and I was looking forward to a visit; there is so much to be
talked over — millions of things to be said.
Then I found he wasn't much of a conversa-
tionalist. I had to draw him out. Now, since
I had entered the writing game, I thought I

should write about extraordinary happenings, so I had written a small sketch of our first meeting. When one is bitten by the writing bug, love and every other human hope and wish must take a back seat; and every person with whom the writer comes in contact must expect to listen to the latest effort. So I read mine to him, and as I read, I watched him, and I thought I was getting him with my writing; but before I finished, he was on his knees in front of me, kissing my hands, and while I had hungered for years for just this sort of treatment, still I was disappointed. I wanted a companion, not a lover. He said, 'I just can't help loving you,' and gathered me into his arms and rained passionate kisses on my throat. Now, if I were D. H. Lawrence, I could write two pages of emotions here, but I will only say that my tendon of Achilles lies in my throat. I started to melt into his arms, when whatever it is that looks after and rules me came to my aid, and I pushed him away, saying, 'Either stay — and I want you to stay — and keep your hands off me, or go.' I don't know how he looked; I couldn't look at him, but he said, 'I cannot be with you and not fondle and caress you.' These old, old words — I didn't know that in these days they were remembered.

They almost finished me; still, with the aid of whatever it is, I said, 'Then go.' 'If I do, I will never come back.' As he went away into the darkness, I called, 'Adios, amigo.'

CHAPTER XIV

If a man praises me, I think he shows good judgment — and wonder what he wants; if he criticizes me, I think him jealous.

A. E.

As my book came to an end, so did my strength; I was soon unable to go after my groceries, but still able to steal roses. A woman who lived near discovered that I was sick and wanted to help me. Everywhere I've been in Colorado, New Mexico, Arizona, and California, I have employed the best doctors and none could do anything for me. I can give you the disposition, dress, and bedside manner of many leading physicians in four States. My neighbor talked me into having a faith-healer. He came late at night; I was in bed doubled up in a knot, with every muscle and nerve tense — even the very marrow in my bones was congested; I was not breathing much nor speaking — just gasping and sweating.

He came in and took off his hat; then removed his kid gloves slowly, pulling each finger carefully to place, then arranged them almost tenderly in the fold of his hat. All this done, he drew up the rocker and sat down carefully, pulling at his trousers so as not to break their creases. I watched every move because this was new to me, and I didn't want to miss anything — if I were entering the gates of Heaven, I'd look to see what kind of hinges they had! He wasn't especially good-looking, and seemed rather like an embittered saloon-keeper. He said nothing, only looked at me through half-closed eyes, then at his hands, folded over his stomach, Buddha-wise. He sat and sat, then almost whispered, 'Peace — Peace.' But, for me, there was no peace.

Then, mentally, I blamed myself. 'It is your fault — because it will not work. It works for other people and would for you if you had faith enough and would believe and help!' I tried to repeat the Lord's Prayer to myself; I raised on an elbow and wiped the sweat that was dripping into my eyes. I must have been a pitiful object, but this healer showed no human interest. A long time he sat, then he left — left without giving me one encouraging word or patting me on the shoulder, or so much as asking if he could hand me a drink of water; left me sick and alone as no man I had ever known would have left a dog. Then I mingled tears with the sweat and prayed to die. I held my breath — what little I had — to see if this would do it; I tried swallowing my tongue, as I had read in R. L. S.'s 'Kidnapped,' that it could be done. But I couldn't make a go of it; my tongue always had been unruly. Finally — it was toward morning — I thought I was really dying, and while I was glad, still I wanted some one with me. So, whenever I heard footsteps on the street, I called and called; none heard me — a good thing, too, I expect, as travelers in that part of town at three in the morning probably would not have been particularly proficient in ministering to a dying woman.

Daylight found me alive, and that's about all. Later in the day my neighbor came, and I had her get a real doctor. The first thing he did was to throw my roses out, then he gave me morphine, and I passed out. They sent for my sister. How glad I was to see her, with her calm, beautiful face and quiet and efficient way! As soon as I was able to go, she took me home with her. Before leaving, I paid the healer the seven dollars which he asked for his demonstration.

I did not go to my sister's home, but rented a small shack near her. When I'm sick, I'm like an animal and want to be alone. Here I lived all summer. Ruth carried my meals to me, and many nights I have heard her walking around the shack, listening to see if I were all right. When I was able, I used to creep to the door and sit there watching the tall pine trees, and wish that I, too, like Joyce Kilmer, might write a poem about trees; or I wished that one of the passing cars might stop and my late lover get out and visit me. I was very subdued and would have received him in quite a different manner.

I was disgusted with writing, and wrote Mrs. Cassidy to return all the letters and I would destroy them. She replied, saying they were going to Europe that winter, and that while in New York she would see an editor and get his opinion. Of course I never really could have burned the letters, but I did bury them deep in my heart and in the bottom of my trunk. I didn't want to worry any more about it. When cooking, I had learned that if I had a poor batch of bread, instead of worrying and working over it, the best thing to do was to make away with it, either by burning or by burying. Once I did bury a batch, but not very deep; of course, I neither confided nor consulted with the Boss as to the wisdom of this, and what was my surprise next day to see the Boss, the men, and the supervisor gathered around a huge white mushroom pushing its way through the dirt. It was my bread, which, after all, had decided to rise.

In the fall, my sister, her children, and I went to Berkeley. All my life I had longed to see the ocean, and had promised myself that if I died without seeing it, there was the first place I'd fly, providing, of course, I was the flying kind. Now I was in sight, sound, even smell of it, and still was not able to visit it. My sister did take me across the bay, almost lifting me on the street cars and up the steps.

As soon I was able, I started for Colorado and my daughter. Going through Arizona, I thought I probably should not pass that way again, so I girded on my armor and decided to see the Grand Canyon if I died in the attempt. We arrived in the morning and stayed all day. I held on to rails, and pulled myself up steps, and rested often. On one bench a man and woman were sitting with their backs to the canyon. He was peevishly cutting his finger-nails; she was writing and addressing postcards — a huge pile. She held one up and blew on the fresh writing, then read aloud: 'You will see where we are. The canyon is sublime and awe-inspiring in its grandeur and immensity. Wish you were here.' And her companion said,

'I'm damned glad she ain't.' Then I walked away as far from the crowd as I could, and sat on a rock in the shelter of the trees; and we visited, the canyon, my soul, and I. When I'm with Nature I want to be alone, and I am such a part and oneness with it that I could no more describe it and my reactions to it than I could describe my right hand and my feeling toward that.

I sat there a long time, and left strong thened and refreshed. As I returned, I saw, at a bend in the road, a man standing on the rim of the canyon. He was a large man dressed in expensive riding-trousers which were held up by a belt with many silver conchos. A three-gallon hat and silver-studded cuffs completed the outfit. Then he turned, and as sure as you're born it was Irvin Cobb in the flesh — quite a lot of flesh, too. Irvin Cobb, his neck encircled with a gay handkerchief pulled through a carved bone ring. But there was something wrong — he was without his cigar. But there must be times, I thought, when Irvin isn't smoking.

Now I am very fond of Irvin Cobb, and I was thrilled at meeting him, and I was determined to talk to him. Thoughts raced through my mind — 'What would one say on meeting a celebrity standing on the edge of the Grand

[229]

Canyon?' Even Emily Price Post has no answer. He was leaving. It was now or never; then I almost tremblingly said this bright thing — 'Do you live here?'

He turned as though I'd stuck a pin in him — 'No, I live on a ranch a mile from here.' He looked me up and down and walked away.

Now I knew Irvin Cobb was given to such pleasantries as this, because if there were a ranch within a mile of the canyon it stood on edge. Still, I knew this was not he, because Irvin, I felt sure, never gave any woman — sick or well — the cold look as he left that this man gave me.

At noon I ate only a lunch, planning on a grand splurge at dinner. (To tell the truth this whole trip was brave — or foolish — of me with my money running so low.)

The woman who that evening at El Tovar ushered me to a table used discernment as she placed four interesting women together. I was one of them. I did not learn who any of the others were, but each was some one. How I enjoyed it!

During the meal my supposed Irvin Cobb strode gloomily in and was seated alone at a small table. I asked if any of these women knew who he was. One of them did. He was

James Swinnerton, the artist, who, I think, humorously draws 'Little Jimmy' and 'Kiddies of the Canyon Country.' My companion went on to say that he had a complex against women. Just my luck!

I met my daughter in Denver. She was riding the high tide of popularity, having just had several poems accepted; also had won a place in an international sonnet contest and had won a state-wide speaking contest against several men. This last was held in the Denver Auditorium. I feared for her; flattery is such a sweet dope, making many addicts, who suffer dreadfully when it is denied them — which is soon. I believe in all due praise, but too much is ruinous. No one could have been prouder, nor more pleased than I; still I did not enthuse — only urged her to keep her feet on the ground. Always I have made myself and my children miserable by trying to train them, trying to fit them for life, not caring how troubled we were at the time if I could only make them stronger in the battle of life. Now I didn't want it ruined by the flattery of foolish women.

The next day a reception was given for Neita by a wealthy friend of hers. I was among those present. I'd been in a good many houses and in lots of homes, but this was my first time in a residence; and I was disappointed. I was not dressed as well as I should like to have been — still, not bad. I was introduced as Neita Carey's mother, which pleased her — she said this was the first time she had not been known as Anne Ellis's daughter. I was not impressed. The food and flowers did not compare with Saguache's food and flowers. Here was the same 'Gab, Gobble, and Git' crowd that I had been used to; they were no better-dressed or mannered; they were no more interesting or informed. Even the fireplace was acting as mine did on occasions — erratic, belching smoke and soot into the rooms. I bet the hostess, who was fuming, that with an old box and a cup of kerosene I could fix it. And, oh, my — it made her mad!

I had always dreamed of receptions given in honor of myself or my children, and now, I found, like many things in life, the dreams were less trouble and sweeter than the realization; besides, they are cheaper and leave no bad taste in the mouth.

To my mind women bootleggers and society women are of the same breed — courageous, tireless, strong physically, ever pushing forward, never daring to relax; both, to gain their ends, giving up many more worth-while things. What wonderful pioneer women they would have made, using their strength, will, and ingenuity to develop a new country!

We went on to New Haven, Colorado, where my son-in-law was Principal of a consolidated school. This was in the dry-farming country, where there are no hills, no trees — only windmills to break the landscape. Here were the Indian-beset plains that, when a small child, I had passed over three times in an ox-drawn wagon.

As I lay in my bed, watching the wind-blown tumbleweeds either coming or going, seeming at a distance like lumbering buffaloes or lurking Indians, I wondered if many times they might not, along with the mirages, have deceived and frightened my mother.

I had heard nothing from my book, and I was willing, as a girl once wrote in my autograph album, to 'Be good, sweet maid, and let who *can* be clever.'

None of the time was I well, and just after Christmas one day, I was sitting up in bed reading Eugene O'Neill's 'Emperor Jones,' when, in a moment, I fell over upon the pillow, very ill. Neita, who was teaching in her husband's place — he also was ill — ran in from the school bus and said, 'Oh, Mamma, today I hoped you would get out in the sun; it is warm and mild.' And I, through my tears, said, 'I'm sick, and I don't believe I will ever get out in the sun again.' Now, when I admit I'm ill, I am. I was running a temperature of 105° right then. As the night drew on, Jack was very bad and I no better, and Neita, after doing all she could for us, went for help a mile to the nearest neighbor's. We had no telephone. There was never a word out of her as she started through the dark, the snow, and the cold, with the wind almost whipping her off her feet, showing that her grandmother's blood still went on.

She telephoned to Sterling for a doctor. He came twenty-five miles, and found us both very ill with flu and, to make Jack's more interesting, he also had mastoid trouble.

During this long hard time a letter came from Mrs. Cassidy. I was so weak it had to be read to me. She said she had taken the letters to a publisher, and that they had passed two readers and had gone to the editorial council, and that she felt very hopeful and would write as soon as she knew the final verdict. But when one is as low as I, worldly hopes and ambitions seem very trivial, and one thinks, 'Why all this strife and struggle?' Then, with the return of life comes hope, and this letter was read many times and was something to cling to.

There came another letter from Mrs. Cassidy, saying that the publishers liked the manuscript, but could not accept it as it was, and suggested that it be rewritten in narrative form. This, at that time, seemed a big job.

As I grew stronger, I thought I'd try something in the short-story line. So, as I imagine a good many more have done, I wrote something for the 'True Stories Magazine,' because McFadden advertised that no experience was necessary; I felt this was just my line. My effort never got by McFadden's censoring board and was returned without a word. So then I jumped from 'True Stories' to the 'Atlantic Monthly.' Again it was returned, but with a nice letter telling me it was 'too sad' and not 'significant' (my first meeting with that word), and that they hoped this would be the 'precursor' of other things for them.

CHAPTER XV

As I walk, as I walk,
The universe is walking with me;
Beautifully it goes before,
Beautifully on either side;
As I walk, I walk with beauty.
                    MARY AUSTIN, *Indian Marching Song*

IN the spring I went home to Saguache with the job facing me of rewriting the book — an especially hard job, as I had no idea just how to go about it. Still, it was good for me to have had that to think about, because those were troubled times.

All summer I was ill; I had not enough strength even to cook my own meals. I had no faith in my writing; however, I did it for the pleasure it gave me. I had decided to leave Saguache that winter, so I arranged my house for renting. It was really a breaking-up of my home — the only real home I'd ever had — a sad business.

It seemed a long time since I had seen Earl. After two years he still had the same job, a job in which there was no advancement and not much more than a living. It seemed he was started on that long hard road of job-hunting.

He was engaged to a lovely girl, with nothing in sight to get married on. The old, old struggle I had wanted to save him from.

Then one day he got off from his work and was coming to see me. How pleased I was! How I held myself up from table to cupboard, and from cupboard to stove, cooking all the things that I knew he liked; and, so far as I could, killing the fatted calf! After a time I was ready and waiting. I waited long past the time when he should have been there, then I knew something dreadful had happened — I can sit and vision the most unheard-of calamities happening to my children. I tried to eat, but everything was tasteless and dry in my mouth.

Then came a neighbor saying Earl had telephoned a message to me from Salida; that when he was ready to start to Saguache, he had changed his mind in a second, and, instead, started for Fort Collins to work his way and finish college. And, you know I was glad.

That November I left for Santa Fé, where I intended to rent a place as cheaply as possible and rest and rewrite the book. I found a house owned by a native woman and rented it for ten dollars per month. It was one large room furnished with a small range, a table, a sanitary couch — called 'sanitary' because that's about all the good that can be said of it — two chairs, a dresser, and a lovely old set of drawers.

At one time Mary Austin, Stephen Graham Phillips, and other notable people had lived in this same room, and I hoped that some of the atmosphere might cling, but, if it did, it was chilly. An ultra-modern artist had moved out to let me move in, leaving on the wall a drawing of two figures, male and female — not so modern, however, but that you could tell what they were up to.

Conditions, according to people who have never tried it, were ideal to make genius burn. I was sick, among strangers, short of money, lonely and cold, and, to round out the picture, infested with mice — little mice, big mice, in-between mice — all kinds of mice except the afraid kind. They climbed up and dropped down and ran over and under everything!

One day the last straw was piled on. I had gone round and round with a stove which smoked and refused to draw. This stove had been moved in and set up by two Mexican women who had thrust a too-small pipe into the chimney, then, to make it fit, had filled in around it with mud. All day it had smoked while a Mexican woman, with a cigarette hanging out of the corner of her mouth, had crept around on her knees pushing a pan of muddy water before her and pretending not to understand a word I said, especially when I suggested that she shake a rug which a former tenant's dog had used for various purposes.

I signed to her, 'See how the stove is smoking!' She only wiped her eyes, shifted her cigarette, then wiped her nose on the back of her hand, and looked up and sniffed, as much as to say, 'Yes, what are you going to do about it?'

I let her creep — she must have been working by the hour. Finally, I decided that I might just as well kill myself working as to be smothered with smoke. So I dashed water on the fire, then climbed upon a chair and dug the mud out, letting it fall where it would. I jerked the pipe out, and found that, rather than pull the stove forward, those women had pushed the pipe right up against the back of the chimney.

The creeper looked reproachfully at the mud, soot, and ashes, and at me; while I urged and shoved her out the door, I repeated, 'Vamose! Vamose!'

Later I washed, dressed, and went to a

near-by grocery for provisions and rat poison. When I went in, the woman, before she even took my order, brought me a chair and a glass of water. I must have looked dreadful, but was still going on my nerve.

When the groceries came, the boy piled them all on the table — there was no cupboard till I manufactured one.

Late that night a Mexican man came to fix the ceiling, which was very high. He was building an adobe house in the yard. All day I had watched him and knew he was tired. So when he came to look the job over, I motioned and talked loud, using all the Mexican I knew, and asked him if he didn't want me to make the paste for him. He grinned, said 'Bueno,' and left. I tottered around, holding myself by the table, the stove, and chairs, and opened the sack of flour and made a big pot of paste.

Then my friend returned. In one hand was a roll of paper, in the other, a steaming bucket of paste! He cut his paper, then motioned to me that he wanted the table. I said, 'No — no, you can lay the paper on the floor and spread the paste' — and I went through all the motions, which didn't convince him in the least. He still insisted on the table. Then

I talked loud, and again showed him he could just as well use the floor. Respectfully he listened, then started to pile the groceries on the floor. I gave up. When the table was empty, he took it over under the place which was to be mended and on top put a rickety chair, then with his paper climbed the tottering affair. I went over and stood in front of the dresser — if he came down, I wanted him to land on me because, if the mirror broke, I just couldn't stand seven years' bad luck.

He finished and left me in the midst of mud, ashes, soot, strips of paper, paste, and groceries. To all this I added a Russian touch by putting poison on buttered bread and left it enticingly around for the rats — and so to bed.

For days I worked, and finally it all came straight — it always does. I was cozy in my room decorated with my curtains and pictures. Each day I laid out my material, preparatory to rewriting the book, but I never wrote a line — I couldn't. I was living in a literary neighborhood, too. Next door lived Arthur Davidson Ficke, the poet, and his wife, Gladys Brown, the sculptor. I heard that H. L. Mencken married them. However, I did not hear this from them, because I never met either of them. They never even knew I was there, and I was never well enough to go over and let them meet me.

To make it harder for me, at this particular time they had, as a guest, Edna St. Vincent Millay, who was putting the finishing touches on 'The King's Henchman,' but, watch as I might, I never got to see her. Every day I did see, dancing on her line, flesh-colored stockings, and if there ever was a time when Edna could say,

> 'My candle burns at both ends,
> It will not last the night;
> But, oh, my foes, and, oh, my friends,
> It gives a lovely light ' —

she certainly was not doing it in Santa Fé.

Just to show how ill I was: Mary and Rafaelita were giving a Spanish supper in Rafaelita's new house. They were to have a home-talent Mexican orchestra and serve thin soup with little balls of ground meat in it, and coleslaw made of blue cabbage (I don't know the name of any of the dishes and I couldn't spell or pronounce them if I did); tortillas of blue corn meal piled in layers with chopped onions and a tomato sauce red-hot with chile between and over the layers; also chile con carne and Mexican beans, and a pudding made of bread crumbs, raisins, and cheese, served with a

sweet sauce; also tiny half-moon pies filled
with jam and fried in deep fat.

As a special inducement, Mary told me that
Witter Bynner was to be there, that he was
always the life of the party, and before the
evening was over he would be the whole show,
singing and dancing, all in Mexican. As
a further inducement, she said there was another bachelor invited, a millionaire. This
was interesting, and I naturally asked his age.
Mary thought around forty. That was young
for me; still, I had heard of various successful
marriages where the wife was older than the
husband. And I planned to go, and even dress,
when I couldn't walk across the floor. Then
I gave it up, knowing that it would kill me to
sit still when Witter Bynner and the others
were dancing, and I sat resentfully in my
window and listened to the 'sounds of revelry
by night' and missed meeting a millionaire
who is now Senator Bronson Cutting from
New Mexico.

That was a bad time. I was so lonely.
There was nothing to read, and I was not able
to read it if there had been; and never leaving
me for one moment was the growing thought
— 'What to do? What to do?' I find this in
my diary:

'*Nov.* 12. Asthma pretty bad. I try not to worry — it may be from dusty rugs. I wish to God I was either able to make myself a home or that I had one, or that I could pass on. As it is now, I look and feel like a Mexican's chicken — and there is no more God-forsaken sight.'

'*Nov.* 20. Still fighting with myself — one side rebelling at fate, or whatever it is. Oh, the dreadful loneliness! My more sensible side telling me, "You are not so bad off — maybe there is hope yet." The other side breaks in — "That's just it. I have gone on hope for a lifetime, now I am too old to have all those things hoped for." "Oh, well," the other side answers — it knows it will win in the long run — it has to — "Get down to writing or to anything that will get your mind off your troubles." The other side, more subdued now, "If I only knew I could write." "You can try, can't you?" "No, I can't even try."'

Then one night, I had a spell — a tantrum, a temperamental fit. Now I have no patience with people who have spells, and I find that a child or grown-up who throws a fit does it before an audience and to gain some selfish end.

I had no audience, and I certainly could gain nothing. Anyway, I screamed and cried and sobbed and threw myself on the bed and cut

up generally. If I had staged this performance
in front of a husband, there probably would
have been a doctor called and a diamond ring
might have been in evidence. This demonstration was all caused by so innocent a thing as
a magazine picture of a woman riding on a surf
board. Now to ride a surf board was not one
of my ambitions, but there were many things
I did want to do, and when I saw that picture
I thought, 'You can never do that, nor climb
a mountain again, nor travel — nor anything
— you are nearing fifty — and ——' And then
I threw the fit.

Mary Austin's home, Casa Querida (dear
house), was just up the hill from where I lived,
and I put in hours at my window watching her
house, hoping to catch a glimpse of her. Mary
Austin is a very great woman. She will die, I'm
afraid, before we realize how great. And how
I longed to meet her! Both Mary Borrego
and her daughter, Rafaelita, knew Mary
Austin very well, and we often talked of
her.

One day shortly after my spell — which
hadn't helped me to any great extent —
Rafaelita said, 'I saw Mary Austin in town
today and told her about you, and she said

that she may come to see you.' Here I copy from my diary:

'*Nov.* — Rafaelita told me Mary Austin was coming to see me, and was I too excited? Anyway, I stayed awake for a long time, then I slept. Then wakened — and something had happened to me. I was exalted — scarcely breathing — very comfortable — and lifted from all care. I even thought, "Then will I not be interested in human things again?" Then I thought, "This might be death and, if it is, it is lovely." Then — I don't know why — I wondered if Mary Austin might not have sent me a message and I wondered if there are great things I know nothing of. All day an old song that my mother used to sing has been running through my head: "Oh, stream of life eternal, flow in and make me free, so nothing can defile me from all impurity."'

'*Nov.* 21. It should be written in red ink! Mary Austin came to see me — and the other night she did send me a message! A new life is opened to me. She gave me this, "I am resting in the presence and the power of the Infinite. Subjective mind and health abundance and fulfillment are manifesting for me." I am so full of thoughts I have no words.'

Mary Austin paid me another visit. That

time she asked me to read some of my manuscript to her. This I did tremblingly, but I had only read a little when Mary Borrego came in, I think much to Mary Austin's relief. Somehow I was not able to follow up this acquaintance. Months afterward I wrote her a note — a flippant sort of a note (the more I feel, the more flippant I am), which deserved no answer and got none.

Each day I grew weaker, and then I got so that I wasn't even able to make my fire. Mary, before she left for work, came and made it. I was scarcely able to cook my meals or to keep my fire going. I used to lie awake nights and wonder if I'd be able to lift the ashes next morning — if I didn't, they would pour onto the floor, and I, no matter how badly I feel, must have things clean. Then Mary told Mrs. Knox Taylor about me, and never after did I lack a friend. She came often and brought books, flowers, food, and, best of all, visited and encouraged me, and whenever everything else failed, she told me I had beautiful hands, lady hands.

Then a day came when I was downright ill. Somehow in counting my money I had made no allowance for doctors and, count it as I would, I could only manage for a few months and leave enough for burial expenses; and with me it was a point of honor to have enough of my own to pay that last bill.

But if you get sick enough, you stop counting money. So I rapped on the window to a passing Mexican and had him call a doctor. Dr. Foster came, and must have been reading recent advertisements because he nonchalantly lit a cigarette and said, 'You belong in the hospital where you can be cared for'; and not even giving me time to dress, he took me to Saint Vincent's. When we were packing my bag — the doctor did most of it and, because of being a bachelor, was very proficient — I threw in part of my manuscript and a pencil — and the doctor grinned.

It was a lovely, peaceful time at Saint Vincent's and I relaxed and rested —- but did not write except in my diary, from which this is copied: 'As the winds of chance lift the fabric of life from the seamy side, I catch glimpses of a lovely right side.'

Then Carl Sandburg came to town and I couldn't see him — and, oh, how I wanted to! I'd just finished reading his 'Life of Lincoln' — and how I wanted to see the man who wrote it! I could only lie there and watch out the window and think each passer-by might be

he. Then, to cap the stack, Lady Diana
Manners came to town. Now I *was* mad — to
be so near seeing a lady and not to!

I stayed in Saint Vincent's longer than
I could afford to; I paid my bill and prepared
to leave, but the doctor made some excuse so
that I did not go for two days or three or five.
I was frantic at spending so much money, and
each day told the doctor, 'Today I must be
leaving.' Each time he made some excuse;
then one day I said, 'Today I *am* going.'
I ordered a taxi and asked a nurse to bring my
bill to me. I waited; no one came with the bill,
and I could see that taxi waiting. I rang my
bell — it wasn't answered. Again I rang.
A calm Indian nurse answered. I told her
I wanted my bill in a hurry; she said, 'All
right' — you don't get much out of any nurse,
nothing at all from an Indian one. No one
came. The taxi waited — so did I — and
again I rang the bell. Then — sweet Sister
Mary Francis came in, almost embarrassed,
nervously clasping and unclasping her hands
in her big sleeves. She smiled and went to the
foot of the bed. I said, 'I am waiting for my
bill.' Then she said, 'There is no bill at this
time.' (Oh, I cried then.) 'Sometime when
you are more able, and if you care to, you can

pay us.' How I cried! Through my tears I said, 'But I can pay you — I want to pay you'; and Sister Mary Francis went on, 'It is just before Christmas, and we want to do this for you; it is a small Christmas gift.' Small? — and I left, bathed in tears and wreathed in smiles.

CHAPTER XVI

Trader Horn expressed my feelings when he said, 'I am bearing philanthropy since I began with the book — I sure can throw it off the chest. Aye, there's something in writings, like armor, to the feelings.'
And, 'The hope that comes from a literary horizon is of a breed harder to kill than most.'

A. E.

I WENT through another round of cold, sickness, and loneliness. The day after Christmas I had taken the covers from my bed preparatory to making it, and was resting before replacing them, when a shadow passed my window; it was followed by a knock. I called, 'Come in,' being too weak to walk to the door. Another knock came, and I shuffled to the door and opened it. I was looking straight into the eyes — big, bright, blue eyes — eager eyes — of a white-haired, handsome man. He was rather poorly dressed, but wore his clothes with an air. One might have thought him a Shakespearean actor down on his luck (I've read about them). I started to tell him that I didn't want to buy anything, when it came to me and I said, 'Is it you?'

It was my father, whom I had not seen for thirty-five years — my faun-like father, artistic, lazy, musical, selfish, irresponsible, irrepressible, changeful, childlike, and charming, a man who had been married three times — and each wife had paid the wedding expenses and was glad to do it. He was a man admired by friends — a man without enemies.

Always dramatic, he was hurt and disappointed that I did not throw myself into his arms and say, 'My father — my father!'

I invited him in, and, with the materials at hand, prepared lunch for him. We were constrained — more so than if we had been strangers. He wanted to talk of his latest project, which was lecturing on archæology; and he could do it well, too, but very likely by the next evening he would be giving banjo lessons. I wanted to tell him of my children, who were, of course, his grandchildren, and about their children, his great-grandchildren; but he never had been interested in any children, not even me, his only child. But I kept silent, only talking of abstract things. Without coming any closer together, without understanding each other any better, we parted, never to meet again in this world.

After Christmas I was so much worse that I had to give up my room and go to a nursing home, fully expecting to be able to go to work by the first of April. I was in bed all winter — rather hopeless — worse by spring; not doing nor wanting to do anything — when one warm day, with green things springing up along the Santa Fé River, I looked up to the hills 'Whence cometh my strength and my endurance.' But none came — I was at last sunk. I got out of bed, trying my legs to see if I could possibly make it to the river, where I intended to dig up and eat wild parsnips. This is a sure and dreadful death, but I could suffer no more. I felt I could go through with it if I returned to bed, resting and gathering strength for the short walk.

Then Miss Duggan, my nurse, brought the mail — a letter from Neita, saying, 'Today I re-read one of your short stories. I think you might do something with it, it sounds arty.' Right then I gave up the parsnip idea. Suppose I could write? It was worth trying — I would struggle on. I did, but I found it impossible to write.

Miss Duggan rented her house, and I found another place where I stayed for one month. Then Neita and her family came to be with me for the summer. All of us were planning on spending the following winter in Arizona. Then the Cassidys returned from Europe, but

I was so ill I made no effort to see them. One day I thought I was dying, and I was glad — I could feel my heart beating fainter and fainter, and I was careful not to revive it. Then I thought, 'Shall I call Neita and tell her good-bye, and leave some instructions? No' — I thought — 'I'll die in peace. I've been instructing her for thirty years, and if she can't go on it's just too bad.' And I thought, 'How lovely death is — no more worry over where I'm going, nor what I'm going to do — no more thought over jobs for myself or any of my family, no more managing or planning, no more moves — wandering-jewing it from place to place — no more fighting cold — no — where I was going it would very likely be warm!' At this I laughed, and came out of it!

One day Neita went up to the Cassidys' and when she returned, she almost ran in. 'Why, Mamma, do you know there were several people there, and all they talked of was your book! Mrs. Cassidy said that the editor said wonderful things of it — only it has to be worked over — and that you must start right away.'

New life — or was it hope, which is life? — seemed to run through me.

So I got the original letters from Mrs.

Cassidy which she had taken to Paris with her
and on into Africa. I had no carbon of the first
five chapters or letters. I worked them over
and wrote the chapter headings. Life was
better — I went to the table for my meals and
was almost human.

Early in the fall, Neita and her family left
for Phœnix, and I was to follow as soon as they
were located. I dreaded it for all our sakes.
I had been compelled to do without many
things in life, but independence was not one of
them. To live successfully with one's children,
one must submerge one's own individuality,
and — I'm not much of a submerger.

When Neita left, I went to a boarding-
house and worked steadily on the book. One
night, lying awake, instead of counting and
recounting my money, trying to see a way out,
I did some constructive thinking; I was fed up
on the progress of the book. It had been three
years since it was written, and it was still
hanging fire. So I gathered up the whole
works — what Mrs. Cassidy had and what
a friend of ours was typing for nothing — and
sent it to a typist in Albuquerque. This was
a bold gesture, since my money was running so
low, but I was determined to know whether
I was a writer or whether I wasn't.

One Sunday there was great excitement in the boarding-house. Lindy was coming to town — every one was going out to see him. No one asked me to go. I was sitting in my room eating alone when a young boy passed the window. I called and asked if he was going to see Lindy, and when he said he was, I said, 'How is it for me to go with you?' We went in a Ford coupé, just touching the high places, and I saw Lindy, and I was not disappointed. I sat on the Capitol steps and could have almost touched his strong, lean, long-fingered hand. He really looked like a young eagle as he gazed out over the clamoring crowd.

Another day — a troubled day — the Armstrongs came to Santa Fé, and to see me. We visited one afternoon, and I don't now remember whether or not I told Mrs. Armstrong how troubled I was. Anyway, a few days after they left, I received a letter from her containing a check and asking — almost urging — me to accept help from them until I might regain my health.

This hurt. Still, I was very glad to know that I had friends like the Armstrongs — the Government bread cast on the waters eleven years before was returning in the way of cake.

In November, I left Santa Fé, stopping off in Albuquerque to rush the final typing. I was going to see that manuscript mailed before I ever left New Mexico. On November twenty-first it started toward New York, and I toward Phœnix, Arizona.

I went into a local sanatorium for a few days and later I moved to a desert sanatorium. If I should compare all my hard times, I believe those months on the desert were the worst. True, I was being provided for and I should not have worried about that — but I did. Then, too, I had given up; I knew that I could never work again. I couldn't even read my hopeful bracers, such as:

'One who never turned his back, but marched breast
     forward,
  Never doubted clouds would break,
Never dreamed, though right were worsted, wrong
     would triumph,
  Held, we fall to rise, are baffled to fight better,
          Sleep to wake.'

No. I pasted in my diary the following by Josephine Johnson:

'I am tired of being patient, I am tired of resignation,
I am sick to death of waiting for a joy that never comes.
I am tired of stingy half loaves, I am tired of imitation,
I am tired of taking other people's crumbs.

Let us once, O soul, be truthful, let us fling aside con-
    cealment —
While we take our fill of sorrow as we never could of
    joy;
It is genuine, abundant — it is ours and not an-
    other's —
Let us once, O soul, taste fullness, though that fullness
    should destroy.'

The most killing, heart-breaking worry was
the watching and waiting for a letter from New
York — a letter that never came. I was afraid
to write to the publishers, because I understood that unnecessary letters only irritate
editors. Then I feared the manuscript had
been lost in transit, and I wrote the publishers
and asked if such a manuscript had been
received. No answer. I waited weeks, and
again wrote, watching and hoping for mail —
the torturing thoughts in my mind running like
caged animals, around and around. Still no
answer. Then I gave up; I was sunk.

CHAPTER XVII

Life is a great adventure; live every hour of it.
Don't be buried until you are dead.

'Tay Pay' O'Connor

At this time a woman who lived in Phœnix and was starting a nursing home heard of me, and was bound to have me for an inmate; she took no tubercular patients, and a sick person in Phœnix who is not a 'T.B.' is a find. So she came out to the desert and almost kidnapped me; took me in and put me into a room with but one window, and that facing a bare wall. I could see only a faint patch of 'that inverted bowl of blue that prisoners call the sky,' and I fell into the bed, pressing my clenched fists against my mouth in order to keep the screams back. Neita came to the rescue, and did everything possible to get me into Saint Luke's, but they drew the line at asthmatics. I don't blame them — I wish I could! Finally we found a 'San' where I went and suffered two months. We concluded that I'd better return to Albuquerque, where we knew I should have good care at a nominal expense. So I prepared for another move — and had to be lifted on the train.

And here is the irony of Fate. The day before I left a letter came from the publishers saying that their failure to answer sooner had been because of a misunderstanding, and that they could not use the manuscript in its present form. I hoped for more, but expected no less. In the same letter was praise, which then I almost resented. When people have struggled till their strength is gone, they don't like for life to prod them up and on.

Still, those were sweet words; the first-hand professional opinion I'd had. As soon as I was settled and rested, I wrote and thanked them for their praise. After a time they answered. Here I will copy from my diary:

'*June* 26. Yesterday I had a letter from S——, a friendly, advising sort of a letter — and the kind I feel sure they seldom write. They praised and found fault. The praise so sweet to me that I've forgotten the faults. If one is struggling, trying to write, such words as these are life-giving: "It seemed to us one of the finest collections of the raw material of literature that we ever saw. Moreover, what we must call the style, was attractive, expressive, and sympathetic." This was not so thrilling and hardest to understand (praise is always so lucid and clear). "The difficulty was simply this: there was no development — no definite and natural beginning and ending, and little variation in the value of the material." Don't I know it? He lost sight of the fact I was writing the true story of my life, and in spite of my wanting it different, wanting development and variation, I did not get it. He went on, "All of the material was detail, splendid detail, but nothing more than that" and my life has been detail, some of it not so splendid. "Perhaps the case would have been better if you had been a little egotistic — if you had made yourself, as people are prone to do, the heroine, and had told your own story in a progressive way, arriving at some point of climax." Oh, yes, how I would like to have had climaxes — to arrive instead of always going somewhere! Now if I had only been writing fiction, I might have made a heroine of myself (never could I for laughing), although I think it is the heroines who do, all their lives, carry on; never arriving, never having climaxes, except birth and death, joy and sorrow, happiness and disappointment. I know just what he meant. I had all the raw material for a book. It's just as if I had piled on a table all the ingredients for a cake; there was the "raw material," but it takes a master hand (such as I have when it comes to cakes — there's egotism for you!) to blend the finished product, to say nothing of imagination, something all good cooks must have, and, I suppose, not a bad asset for writers.'

I wrote and told Mrs. Armstrong that my manuscript had been returned (I think she took my writing with several grains of salt; well, so did I!) and that the publishers had praised it. She answered immediately, telling me to send the manuscript to her and she would have a friend read it. I then advised the publishers to send their copy directly to Mrs. Armstrong.

Then one day I had a telegram — they frighten me so. The friend, Lucy Fitch Perkins, had read it and liked it — oh, I was glad! Later, Mrs. Armstrong wrote that Dorothy Speare had been in Evanston and Mrs. Perkins had given a dinner for her and other artists and had entertained them by reading parts of my manuscript to them, and that they were pleased. So was I, but I had my doubts about asking the opinion of any one just after you'd fed them. I *was* happy, and very, very grateful to Mrs. Armstrong and Lucy Fitch Perkins. The joy of not being useless!

My luck had turned. That spring Earl

graduated from college — my dream realized — and how sorry I was not to be able to attend commencement! — but you can't have everything. The girl to whom he was engaged did go and later wrote me all the details — how handsome he looked, how well he'd done, and how the President complimented him. Earl had the running gears of an automobile, in which he took her home. In Denver he heard of a job that he might get, and, dressed as he was, flannel shirt open at throat, not very smart knickers, bareheaded, and, taking Arline with him and leaving her in the hall to wait, he went and asked for that job. Of course he was asked many questions. One of them was, 'Are you married?' He said, 'No, not yet, but I'm going to be if I get this place. Come out in the hall and meet the girl.' (Earl is like that!) He got the place, and a very wonderful one it is too.

A good many letters went back and forth from Mrs. Armstrong, Mrs. Perkins, Mrs. Perkins's publishers, and myself, and it all took time. The manuscript had to be edited and cut down. It seemed I had enough for almost two books, and Mrs. Armstrong wrote that it would have done my heart good to have heard them when they were deciding what to cut and what to leave. Then the manuscript made several trips between Albuquerque, Evanston, Boston, Michigan; Albuquerque, Boston, New Haven; Albuquerque and Boston. Then, waiting. Writing is a game of waiting, and, unless one is a good waiter, a discouraging game.

Earl was to be married on Christmas Day and I was mad; not hurt — plain mad! All my life I had been a plaything of Fate, often knocked over, and always my leaden balance, like that in a toy, had brought me upright to place again and really smiling, as the fool things do. But now I wasn't smiling. I always had in a way thumbed my nose at Fate and dared it to do its worst — with reservations, however, because Fate really has the 'Indian sign' on me, only I won't admit it. I was fed up on fighting Fate; I wanted to wallop her or it right where it lived and say, 'There, damn you, take that!'

I couldn't go to the wedding — a church wedding, too — and I'd never seen one. Earl was going to wear a tuxedo, too, and I'd never seen one of those either — and there was a reception, and a best man, and bridesmaids, and flowers, and photographs, and food. I was *mad!* I wasn't at all Pollyanna-ish and had no good will toward men, nor anything. Even Neita's presents, which were always a glowing delight and were spread out days before to gladden nurses, maids, and trayboys, did not thrill me; nor Jose's gifts, and the pine boughs she always sent from Bonanza. I was miserable, and enjoying it!

Then a boy came with a telegram:

DEC. 24 — 1928

MRS. ANNE ELLIS,
METHODIST SAN,
ALBUQUERQUE, N.M.
WE HAVE ACCEPTED YOUR BOOK FOR PUBLICATION NEXT YEAR STOP FINAL REVISION NOW GOING ON STOP WITH BEST WISHES FOR THE HOLIDAYS
HOUGHTON MIFFLIN COMPANY

Oh, I *do* believe in fairies! There *is* a Santa Claus — oh, thank God — thank God!

THE END